Praise for *Fourteen Hills*

"Beautifully designed, impeccably edited, *Fourteen Hills*
is one of those handful of literary journals doing the important
work of keeping American writing alive and new."
George Saunders, author of *Tenth of December*

"The journal is something of a collage itself, boasting a variety of
talented writers from San Francisco and around the world."
Jennifer Gomoll, *NewPages.com*

"[*Fourteen Hills*] blends the traditional litmag with
experimental writing in a slick, well-produced journal."
Todd Dayton, *MetroACTIVE*

"Smart, quirky, literate—every piece in this journal gives
the reader a juicy nugget to sink their teeth into, and
something meaty that sticks to the mind's ribs."
David Henry Sterry, author of *Chicken*

Fourteen Hills

Vol.23 No.1

2017

Acknowledgments

Fourteen Hills would like to thank the following individuals and businesses for their help and support in putting this issue together:

Lara Coley
Dirk Petersen
Loria Mendoza

Barbara Eaton
Katherine Kwid
Peter Orner

McNaughton & Gunn
Wendy Juback
Jim Murphy

Fourteen Hills would like to thank the following individuals and businesses for their generous donations to our fundraising events:

The Albatross Pub, Eric Barker, Jen Deering, Delfina Restaurant Group, Samuel McCormick, Other Avenues, St. George Spirits, Christina Urreaga, Yoga Beach, and Workshop

Correction

In issue 22.2, W. P. Osborn's essay "A Wind of Light" was published with an incorrect opening sentence. The following sentence is the version the author intended for publication: "To preclude your thinking from what I am about to say that I am one who on a weekend morning will get on a tee and poke around for three hours on wet grass when he could spend some of that time in a nice warm bed, I will stipulate, and my spouse, who has seen me quote unquote play, can corroborate, that golf—my topic here—is a sport where I can claim no expertise in any aspect, most apparently in driving the ball." *Fourteen Hills* takes full responsiblity for the ungrammatical sentence that went to print and regrets this editorial error.

Credits

Book Layout and Design: Danielle Truppi, Bradley Penner
Cover and Art Design: Danielle Truppi
Copy Editors: Fisayo Adeyeye, Farah Amezcua, Adam Cook, Jack Darrow, Keith Donnell, Alysia Gonzales, Vanessa Hamill, Sofía López, Zoë Marshall, Bradley Penner, Michael Petitte, Emily Pinkerton, Margaret Spilman, Danielle Truppi, Lenore Weiss, Presley Wiseman
Cover Artwork: Bryan Valenzuela, *Tempest Music Take Me Away V.2* (front); *Tempest Music Take Me Away V.1* (back), Ink, Acrylic, Watercolor, Gel Transfer on Arches Watercolor Paper, 40" X 26"

Distribution

Small Press Distribution, Berkeley, California (www.spdbooks.org)
Ubiquity Distributors, Inc., Brooklyn, New York (www.ubiquitymags.com)

ISBN: 978-1-889292-71-7

Fourteen Hills is published by the Creative Writing Department at San Francisco State University, with the support of the Instructionally Related Activities Fund.

THE SAN FRANCISCO STATE UNIVERSITY REVIEW

Vol. 23 No. 1

2017

Bradley Penner
Danielle Truppi
Editors-in-Chief

Emily Pinkerton
PR & Events Manager

Sofía López
Managing Editor

Brittany Smail
Web Manager

Fisayo Adeyeye
Poetry Editor

Margaret Spilman
Fiction Editor

Presley Wiseman
Art Editor
Assistant Poetry Editor

Michael Petitte
Assistant Fiction Editor

Lenore Weiss
Copy Editor

Heather June Gibbons
Faculty Advisor

Editorial Staff

Farah Amezcua | Adam Cook | Jack Darrow | Keith Donnell
Alysia Gonzales | Vanessa Hamill | Zoë Marshall

Fourteen Hills is published twice yearly in San Francisco, California.

Subscriptions

Individual—One year for $17. Two years for $32.
Subscription Renewal—One year for $15. Two years for $28.
Institutional—One year for $30.

Submissions

Writers may submit once per submission period. All submissions are electronic. Submission periods are: September 1 to December 1 for inclusion in the spring issue (released in May) and March 1 to June 1 for inclusion in the winter issue (released in December). All other correspondence may be addressed to the appropriate editor at *Fourteen Hills*, c/o the Creative Writing Department, San Francisco State University, 1600 Holloway Avenue, San Francisco, CA 94132. Details at www.14hills.net.

Contents

Kimberly Grey / Family System 11

MRB Chelko / Worker BE. 12

Dani Blackman / This Is Where You Live Now 13

Krystal Languell / We begin with. 25

Raeleen Kao / There Let Her Lie VIII 26

/ There Let Her Lie XVIII 26

Melissa Carter / Untitled (Ipanema) 27

Kayleb Rae Candrilli / Strike. 28

John Sibley Williams / Then We Will Make Our Own

Demons 30

Lindsay Hunter / Baggies. 32

Krystal Languell / A neighbor stopped. 34

Stephen Haynie / Surveillance 35

Nicole Jost / You, the Accused 44

Lindsay Hunter / Cookies 55

Tyler Kline / Advice from Stevie Nicks on Dreaming 58

Kevin A. Phan / 10 Questions for John Berryman. 59

Michael Trocchia / Dementia. 60

Colleen Louise Barry / excerpt from Badlands 61

Michael Mungiello / The Mother Totem 74

Anna Rotty / Melanie Sleeping 79

Ashley Johnson / Woven. 80

Mia Ayumi Malhotra / Nighttime Feed. 81

Stephanie Dickinson / Big Headed Anna and the Blue Virgin 82

Laura Cesarco Eglin / Insurgencia 86

Jesse Lee Kercheval & Catherine Jagoe / Mutiny (translation) 87

Emily Kendal Frey / All Love Is Good Love 88

Glenn Kinen / Shortcuts 90

Alyssa Lempesis / Nice Parts 105

Bryan Valenzuela / Whether or Not the Bellwether of a Blizzard in

My Brain 106

Kayleb Rae Candrilli / Chew 107

Kristian O'Hare / Dowsing 108

2016 Gina Berriault Award Winner:

Suzanne Rivecca / Feast Days 109

Loria Mendoza / Interview with Suzanne Rivecca 131

Barry Ebner / Untitled 142

/ Walls Series 143

Megan Peak / I Felt the World Cracking 144

Ösel Jessica Plante / Go to the Edge of Giving Then Break

Yourself 146

Lindsay Hunter / In the Dining Room 147

M.A. Vizsolyi / Fuegal Requiem 149

Zachary Doss / The Future of Society 150

Contributor Biographies 155

Fourteen Hills

THE SAN FRANCISCO STATE UNIVERSITY REVIEW

Family System

Kimberly Grey

That we are eased often, into, and from each other means
we have options. Like the body easily deciding when it loves
and when it unloves   an estuary of sorts.
It becomes, source-like,
where all things run. It's so much like that. Anyone
who has a body knows, perhaps it's for biological reasons,
we go (and it's rampant) toward
the thing that unwants us. In fact, I demonstrated it. Once
in a house where nothing loved
me I loved everything back. It was astonishing. The furniture
curled against backbones and those people didn't know,
those people didn't know what to do. So together
we suffered (with a yellowing ease). Even the trees outside were
quiet. I estimate that's all it took, a day, maybe longer—
to become like an erasure. They erased me from that house,
held the curtains open
wider, until the light unshaped my love (not shock-
ingly) into something harder.

Worker BE

MRB Chelko

time first darkens the page   pink and yellow
carbon copies partially detached   what I want
be what I need   the way we had nothing then
and not much now   I mean in the bank   I mean
beneath our feet   the skin thick and muddied
at the shores of our toenails   I bought a new broom
got a first tattoo at thirty   it was the last desk
in the furthest cubicle in the smallest office in
the universe (warehouse)   and it was mine
        and I traveled there beneath the countless arches
                of the big grey interstate and took my lunch outside
                        to a mound of dried concrete painted brilliant
                                yellow cautionary yellow *here I am*   yellow

This Is Where You Live Now

Dani Blackman

Miller needs the park, so every day we go to the park. Every day we hike the hill and lock the strollers at the bench next to the wading pool and wait for the peace that is headed our way. If we close our eyes, we might hear the push of ferries rolling into shore or a pair of transient orcas splashing back below the surface. I still won't close my eyes, so this is what I see: none of the kids has kicked up any dirt yet and the mothers stay quiet with full cups of coffee and smartphones. Most people haven't started their days.

We have a front row seat for when the big kids arrive. Then we'll look closely and imagine what's in store for the boys. Now we stare into the baseball fields and don't have much to say. From a distance we could be twins, but up close anyone can see that Miller is older than I am and not as happy. She hasn't lost the baby weight and I have. She'll always be prettier, but together we could be the prettiest. Together we're a team: I won't spill her secrets and she grants me a place to stay.

Behind the swings, a lanky boy with shoulder-length hair trips an even lankier boy and calls him a tree stick. "Haven't you used that one before?" Miller says.

Some days I love her like a sister, some days I love her like a lover. There've been five days in twelve years of friendship that I've wanted to kill her. She is family and our sons will be brothers.

"Why is it always the weird one who falls?" Miller says and bounces the handle of the stroller to get Nash back to sleep. "Look at him. Glasses, curls, the whole package."

"That could be Hudson one day," I say.

Because Hudson came too early, certain delays are almost a guarantee. Nash arrived on Hudson's due date and via C-section out of fear he'd get stuck in the birth canal. That's how huge Nash was. Or is. We rarely place the boys right next to each other, because it still doesn't seem fair.

"Our boys are beautiful," I say.

"Don't worry," Miller says. "Hudson is too."

It's Friday and the good families are gone. They've hit the highway and are halfway to another state line. They're destined for campfires and lake swims. We study our sleeping boys; we hum different lullabies.

"I feel full-blown boredom setting in," Miller says and shifts to stand behind Nash's stroller. She squats and curls her arms as if she's lifting heavy weights. She passes the time.

She's freed up space on the bench and before I can spread the boys' blankets a girl in a Cinderella dress skips over to sit down next to me. Her dress makes the sound cheap dress material makes. She is a fat Cinderella. She has dimples and chocolate on her chin and more dark stains on the white of her dress. She watches Miller's leg squats and laughs.

"Are you a bad guy?" Cinderella asks.

"Yes," Miller says.

Cinderella screams. Then cries. She kicks Nash's stroller and runs to the bench across from us to throw her head into her mother's jeans and cry some more.

"You can't tell a kid you're a bad guy."

"Why," Miller says. "It's true."

Between the benches, Cinderella's mom slingshots me a look that makes me suck in my stomach.

"Just stop looking at her," Miller says.

"I'm not looking."

"We didn't do anything wrong." Nash is across Miller's torso like a shield.

"The mother's coming."

"Don't look, don't look."

"It's too late," I say.

The mother has guided Cinderella to the safety of the sandbox and has crushed a perfect patch of grass with her ridiculous beige clogs to come and stand over us. She lifts her sunglasses. "You need help," she says into the space between the strollers. "I'm here to help."

We don't correct her. We learn her name is Meri. Not Mary. Meri. We tell her our names and introduce the boys. We now know that Cinderella is actually an Ashley. After Meri takes two fingers to both boys' cheeks I think we're in the clear.

"Are you both," Meri says. And she should just spit out what we all know she's trying to say. "Are you both the mothers?"

"Yes," I say. "Well yes and no."

"We're fine," Miller says.

"Beautiful boys," Meri says.

"We know," Miller says.

"No need to get defensive," Meri says. "I have a boy too. He's just with his father most of the time. My donkey of an ex got him and I got Ashley. That's what the donkey wanted. He didn't stop until he got what he wanted. You know men. Or maybe you don't."

"We should go," I say.

"My house is right over there." Meri points to the biggest three-story box on the block. "Who needs to get caught in the rain? Who wrote that ending? We can have lunch instead."

A few fat raindrops hit my shoulders. "Why not?" I say, because I should be a gracious person. I think about lunch. I won't look at Miller.

When we've secured the boys back in their strollers, we take our space and walk a good fifty feet behind Meri and Cinderella. I decide that's what I'll continue to call her, despite knowing her real name. Meri and Cinderella sing a song we have yet to learn and toss their arms in the air.

"Don't worry," I say to Miller. "I'm not going to tell her anything."

On Meri's couch, Hudson sits on Miller's knee and Nash is on mine. We're mixing things up. We're safe this way. And Meri doesn't get any more guesses. She is in her kitchen boiling water for tea, even though Miller and I declined her offer. Cinderella is on the floor, with her back against Miller's bare legs. She didn't ask permission. But Miller has yet to move.

"Will you read me a story?" Cinderella asks and cranes her neck back to look at Miller.

"I'm not a good reader," Miller says.

"It's true," I say.

"Will you braid my hair then?"

"I guess," Miller says and hands Hudson over.

"How was the sandbox?" I ask Cinderella.

"You should try it," she says. "But make sure you take your shoes off. You need to feel the sand on your feet. That's the whole point."

"Thanks for the advice."

"You're pulling too hard," Cinderella tells Miller and squirms in her princess dress.

Miller twists two strands of hair together and calls it a day. She gives a final yank. "Go take a look kid," she says into the back of Cinderella's head.

"We should go," I say. "It doesn't take this long to make tea."

"She's not making tea," Cinderella says. "It's apology juice."

"What?" Miller says.

"When you drink it, you'll learn how to say you're sorry," Cinderella says. "To me."

Hudson smiles and Nash lets out a series of chuckles. Both boys are all right. Miller wrings a blanket in her hand, but I don't know why she's worried. We spent our twenties taking from strangers.

When Meri returns to the living room, she spreads a light turquoise blanket across the hardwood. "If you want, I can put more pillows down and we can all have some fun on the belly."

"I'm in the middle," Cinderella says.

"Do this for her," Meri mouths when Cinderella turns her back.

"I need a second," Miller says. "I need two."

"Where are you going?" I ask.

"Just the bathroom," she says. "I just need to catch my breath."

"Apologies aren't easy," Cinderella says.

Miller doesn't turn around. The next time I look she's out of my sight. Nash and Hudson crawl around Cinderella who keeps up a conversation with herself and I turn more than once to check for Miller even though I know she's already gone.

"You should go on without her," I say.

"But it's her ceremony," Cinderella says.

"I can say sorry too," I say. "I'm sorry."

It's going to take more than that," Cinderella says.

I drink the apology juice—a sugary, saturated orange slush that takes more than one swallow to get all the way down. I don't gag and I'm only slightly paranoid. I decide that Miller will nurse Hudson until I know we're in the clear.

"You have to finish it for it to work," Cinderella says.

"She'll know if you haven't finished it all," Meri says. "Trust me."

I take down the rest and turn the cup over to let them know I'm done. The boys begin to cry and I'm grateful that I now have a better excuse to leave. "I have to go."

"But what are you feeling?" Cinderella says.

"I'm feeling sorry," I say.

"You should be feeling more."

"I'm feeling really sorry."

"It didn't work," Cinderella says.

"Of course it did," Meri says. "She said she's sorry."

"It was a weak batch," Cinderella says. "We have to do it again."

"I don't think so," I say.

"Come back tomorrow," Meri says. She shoves a crumpled fifty-dollar bill into my palm and keeps her hand over my fist. I feel something I'm unwilling to name. "Come back tomorrow and we'll do it again."

At the apartment Miller has changed into a long tee shirt and nothing else. She sits on the couch with her legs pushed out to the coffee table and closes her laptop when she sees me.

"I could kill you," I say and drop both diaper bags in the middle of the floor. "Do you know how hard it is to walk two strollers down a hill?"

"I couldn't stay," she says. "You know how I get."

"You owe me," I say. "Both boys need to eat."

In the bedroom I hide the fifty in a pair of camping socks I keep in the back of my drawer.

"I'll cook for you tonight," Miller shouts from the living room. "We can play cards."

"You don't really owe me," I say, because I know she can't hear me.

When I return Miller makes room for me on the couch; she likes her arms across my hips while we sit. Besides keeping me full, the apology juice leaves no effect. I already know I'll go back tomorrow.

"Don't let Meri get to you," Miller says. "She's new and shiny and rich. That's it."

"She's legitimately pretty," I say. "She's nice."

"She's a tree stick."

⌒

I spot them as soon as we get to the park—Cinderella is dressed as Cinderella again and is at the top of the slide, ready to land head first into the dirt; she has two or three new stains on her dress. Meri sits on her bench. I wait for her to see me and when she does she calls us over.

"We were looking for you," Meri says.

"Cinderella must be so hot in all of that fake polyester," Miller says.

"You try talking her out of that dress," Meri says. "Every morning it's a battle of wills. And she got the donkey's. But you get what you get when it comes to the kids. You already know that."

"What's that supposed to mean?" Miller says.

"I won't say it," Meri says. "Don't make me say something we don't want to hear."

I want to rip through her throat for making me move close to my fears about Hudson. She's not wrong, and that's what I have to accept. She's just honest, which is just cruel enough.

"My boy." But that's all Meri says.

"We get it," Miller says.

Meri dares us to lose our edge, and asks us to follow her and Cinderella to the pitcher's mound of the baseball field to make sand angels. Miller wheels both boys away. But I'll do what Meri wants.

In the dirt, Meri and I giggle as mindlessly as Cinderella does, and Meri drops another fifty onto my chest. The bill stays in place as my arms stir at my sides.

"You love her," Meri said. "It's not hard to see."

"Everyone does," I say.

"Nash and Hudson will know that soon enough. They'll know your shame."

I push out my arms and legs.

"If there's anything to shield your kids from it's that," Meri says. "Your shame, not theirs. Theirs you won't be able to stop. Theirs you'll cry twice as hard over."

"We don't cry," I say. The sun shoots heat to my shoulders. I can't see Miller and the boys.

"The only time Ashley saw me cry was when the donkey told me what really made him seal the deal," Meri says. "The affair was a given. That was only a matter of time. But when he had me lie on the same sheets he had her in for one last comparison, well."

"I don't know what to say."

"Has she ever made you feel invisible?"

"Yes," I say. I pocket the fifty.

Miller still needs the park, but for four days she stays home. Without Miller, I strap Hudson to my chest and Nash to my back and meet Meri and Cinderella for whatever they've planned for the day. Yesterday, I crouched under a tree for Cinderella's backwards game of tag and listened to Meri play a recording of a song she is composing with Cinderella. She put her phone to my chest. "Hear it from your heart," she said.

Nash clapped for her; Hudson raised his hands.

When Meri addresses the boys, she refers to herself in the third person. *Meri made blackberry pie. Meri has baby pools and new toys. Do you want to go to Meri's for some pie?* The boys aren't yet one, but they get it. They turn their hands in front of their eyes and Meri bounces up and down for peek-a-boo. She is their new game.

Today we're taking it easy, but we're back under the tree. Summer camps have arrived from all over the city and stay divided by different colored tee shirts. Cinderella pulls one of the girls from the purple group and together they skip across the drawbridge.

"Maybe she'll finally make a friend." Meri's hand brushes against the back of my thigh and she doesn't apologize. "Last night I had a sex dream about Big Bird," she says. "I was hot and on my back and finally ready and then there he was, beaking at my neck with his big yellow beak."

"I miss sex," I say, which could be true.

"I was finally ready," Meri says again.

Before I take Hudson to bed, I hold Nash and squeeze each one of his toes. I can tell our days are numbered. That's how it happens with Miller. It happens just like that. Without much left to save us, I find the ball of Meri's cash and give it to Miller, who holds the bills with both hands and counts how much we have.

"I think she's just lonely," I say.

"She's sick," Miller says. "But at least now we'll have a good dinner."

Our steaks arrive fat and bloody, just like we like them. It's the best meal we've eaten in years.

"How much more do you think we can get from her?" Miller asks.

The first guy we fucked for cash was a stranger. He opened his palm and handed us four pills and that was it. When we saw him again the next night, he had more money and more drugs. And he became our thing, a person we met multiple times in multiple bars and hotels, a story we'd often tell friends or new lovers to offer ourselves as the most daring women they'd ever met.

One of the boys cries out in his sleep and we don't have much time left with our meat. We eat from our hands. The juices drip off our chins, but we don't wipe our mouths.

In my mind I shape a small, dramatic scene in which a crowd of mothers forms to watch Miller drop the rest of Meri's money between the benches where we first met. "Take it back," I want Miller to say to Meri. "We don't need it." I'm ready for Miller the strong one again, to draw a line where I can't. But when we arrive at the park, Miller heads straight for Meri and Cinderella. I stay a few feet behind with Nash and Hudson, as if anything could happen, even though I'm completely sure of what comes next.

Miller bends down so her words hit Cinderella's face. "I'm ready to apologize."

So we're off to Meri's again, to dodge the afternoon sun, to eat free lunch, to earn our cash, to make some of this seem right. Today the six of us go as a group, like a blob tottering down the sidewalk, like we're part of a parade for mothers who shouldn't be mothers.

At Meri's house, Nash cruises along the coffee table and Hudson keeps up with the help of Cinderella who has both hands on his back and scoots him forward each time he stops. Minutes later, we eat pretzel sticks and thick, round turkey slices on white bread without crust. The boys eat blueberries and this day might come to some harmony; Cinderella plays kids' tunes on an old record player.

"Where's the apology juice?" Miller asks when the needle lifts.

"It's been over a week," Meri says. "There's nothing left."

"But that's how it happens," Cinderella says. "It's what we've been waiting for."

"It's what we agreed to," Miller says.

"There's wine for the women in the fridge, Ashley," Meri says. "Let her drink that."

"This isn't what you promised!" Cinderella throws herself down to the floor and screams and then screams even louder and doesn't stop.

"I'll definitely take the wine now," Miller says. "You can bring the whole bottle and then go up and do the cellar. You can do them both together, Cinderella."

Without any other choice, Meri forces a timeout and carries Cinderella upstairs. Cinderella bangs on the wall the whole way up and after ten minutes we don't hear her anymore. Nash settles against Hudson and they're back to the floor with their limbs in the air.

Meri returns and pours glasses of wine and drops three-hundred dollars on the table. "Let's do something else," she says and takes off her shirt.

There were more men after the first one. There was a man with a trail of thousands who we followed all the way to Seattle. I get what you're thinking, but we know the boys' fathers. We can even call what we had relationships. But that still wasn't enough incentive to stay. What would that say about us if we'd stayed?

Meri's stomach is tight and trim, without deep purple marks. Without many signs.

Miller stares at the money on the table. "We're not going to fuck you. She doesn't want to fuck you," Miller says to Meri and steps closer to me.

"It's not always about sex," Meri says. "Show me your stretch marks."

"What?"

"Show me how far you've come."

I start at the bottom of my shirt, but Miller stops me. "I'll do it," she says.

Miller unbuttons her shirt and slides her bra up. Meri kneels to get a better look. I pick up both boys. Meri is too close. But Miller will never cry. Tiger attack, Miller's called her stomach before, because that's what it looks like. Miller has too many marks to count. They cross each other. They fold into her skin. They're dark and won't disappear.

"You've really paid," Meri says.

Miller puts on her shirt so her scars are out of sight again.

"You can cover yourself up, but it doesn't matter," Meri says. "This is where you live now."

Miller folds the bills on the table and slides the cash into her back pocket. She takes Nash and I hold Hudson and we walk back to the front door.

"Meri," Nash says. It's as clear as it could be. It stops me and Miller in our steps.

"He said Mama," I say. "That was Mama."

"Mama," Hudson says. And only a second or two behind Nash.

We begin with…

Krystal Languell

(We begin with (an invocation))   (Affiliating with the right god)

((Is respect no more) (than self-defense))

(The diction implies)   (you should know (the reference))

(After means since when do I care)

(Once it's way too late to place blame)

(Only I was encouraged to respond)   (to)   (neighborhood politicking)

(When I had returned from)   (mosquitos and sawdust) (in the piss trough)

(In light (of recent events))   (all balconies rebolted)

(We signal emergency) (crash into a berm)   (pointless)   (without a witness)

(Where did my needle go) (tucked in an envelope)

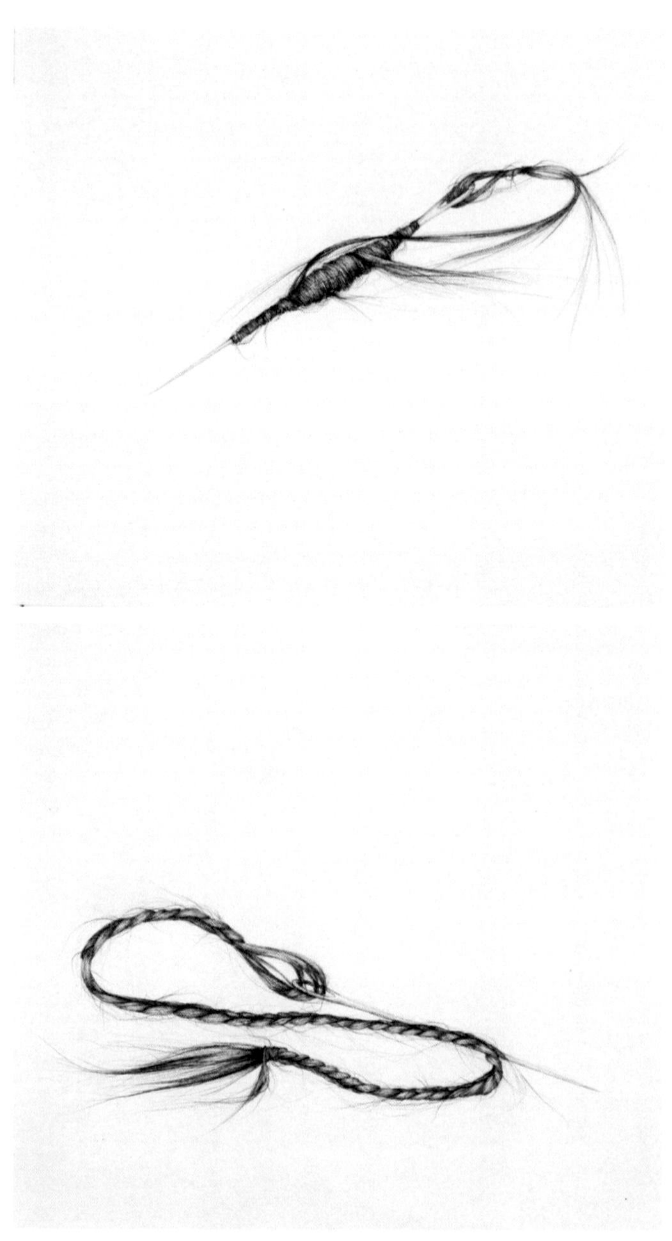

There Let Her Lie VIII (top)
There Let Her Lie XVIII (bottom)

Raeleen Kao
GRAPHITE ON PAPER

Untitled (Ipanema)

Melissa Carter
35MM

Strike

Kayleb Rae Candrilli

My father often tells the story of his electromagmatism
and it's magnetic. He uses his hands to describe the way

an air conditioner can shock—floodwater deep
in the basement—the way a socket can perform

both static and electric. But the story always starts
on the beach that ropes Coney Island. My father sold coke

there but that's not the story. The story is how he understates
absolutely nothing except almost being struck by lightning.

He says *I was the only one around.* But still it bolt-landed just
next to him. What is the third degree if not a near smiting?

Hushed, he told me how his feet smoked up, charred
on the bottoms, a spider web of fire spreading to catch

his soles. The sand, he said, turned to black glass
around him, and my god, he was almost stuck there forever.

He tells me everything as he forces the shock of a 9-volt
onto my tongue. I always swallow and say *thank you*

because I need to be trained in what shocks. So,
when I smoke crack for the first time, see, it's not anything

other than a show of resilience, of living through a "one-time
thing." This business of not dying is inherited. This business

of thwarting the divine is all blood line, DNA, pre-programmed.
And, now, because I put myself in every place he's ever been,

I ride the Wonder Wheel and think about the vastness
of the ocean. I look out onto a roping beach and see how

it can noose—and my father is still there, you know.
He's there, stock still divining rod, cemented in glass.

What is a family if not preparation? I can smell the storm
coming before anyone. I swear I can taste it rolling in.

Then We Will Make Our Own Demons

John Sibley Williams

This is what happens
when no one has set the living room
ablaze in decades.

When mother calls across an empty field
and all her children come running
from the shadows, safely, home

to an abundant plate; every time,
ripe apples and merciless wholeness.
Thighs unbruised even after clenching

the belly of a mare there was no need
to break. When not a series of slaps
but the earth gently folding up upon itself

is what hardens the mountains. When father
was a mountain. And still has not proved himself
otherwise. When lumps of sugar are enough

for kids to learn the names of trees. *This
is a sycamore. Sweet, bloodless sycamore.
Son, this is how you carry moonlight*

into the house. When the bodies
flapping away, half-mast, are all cotton
and glory. Petrifying crows. Harvest.

When your name is less an arrow
pulled from whatever you felt you had
to fell; instead it is a thread dissolving

into a forgotten wound. When all wounds
have hints of birds in them. Sometimes
the whole bird. When the whole damn bird

fits in your eye, and you are nothing but love
for a candle inching closer to the sofa. *Mom,
here it is. Here is the moonlight.*

Baggies

Lindsay Hunter

It was 4:00. The lunch had begun at noon. No one could say that it was still lunchtime. Just seconds ago Cousin Richie had leaned forward, had looked at the algae-green numbers staring out from the cable box, had seemingly absorbed the hour, and had leaned comfortably back in his chair. Stretched his legs out in front of him, admired his long thin toes in his leather sandals, Cousin Richie in shorts and sandals though it was November and there was a glittering of snow out already.

4:01. Cousin Richie crossing his ankles now, raising his plastic tumbler of wine and saying, I could go for another nip, and when the bottle didn't appear before him, saying it again. Aunt Bette, his mother, pushed up from her own seat to fetch the bottle for him, walking hunched and stiff like a cavewoman breaking out of the fossil she'd inhabited for thousands of years.

4:02. One-sixth of the day had now been wasted among this detritus of family. Cousin Richie, unemployed for decades, who had mastered the moist eye and soothing tones of someone who truly listened but never remembered a detail. Aunt Bette, whose mouth resembled an anus, it had to be said. Tight and wrinkled and opening only to spill out turd after turd of meanness. Aunt Bette who said the baby resembled a bottom feeder fish, all startled eyes and bloat, who had hacked and spit into her coffee cup and handed it over like she'd done a favor. Cousin Richie's daughter, Rylee, who said she needed money, had snatched the bills like they'd been stolen from her, and had spent the four hours smoking and pacing and glaring in through the windows from the deck. And Cousin Richie's dog. Boomer. Actually a sweet animal who looked terrified when he wasn't licking his own turgid penis. His red rocket, Cousin Richie called it. His lipstick, Aunt Bette corrected.

4:07. No one had said a word for five whole minutes. Cousin Richie had nodded as if he were listening and understood. The lunch was in danger of stretching into dinner. The world was turning, people were free outside this house. Suddenly the word, the word that could end it all, the Well. . . it burbled forth, no one was sure who said it, but it was spoken and it scattered in the air like a burst sac of spider eggs.

Cousin Richie's face fell, it was clear he had wanted to work this into a dinner and now the jig was up. Aunt Bette went for her purse, Cousin Richie stood to rummage in the various pockets of his cargo shorts. Through the window, Rylee saw and flicked her cigarette, a shooting star that arced and landed, smoking, in a deck chair.

Cousin Richie pulled a fogged, gallon-sized baggie from his shorts. We can't forget our leftovers, he said. Rylee appeared, putting apple slices and an unopened package of sandwich meat underneath her hoodie, it was clear stealing was the only way she understood give and take. Cousin Richie swept the remnants of the veggie tray into his bag, poured the warm ranch dressing over it all, threw in the final three brownies on top. Aunt Bette had few choices. A half bag of sandwich bread, the crumbs at the bottom of the bowl of chips. She aimed her disappointed face around the room, went with the bag of bread, sighed like it was she who'd survived the reaping.

At 5:07 they'd been gone forty-five minutes, the kitchen was clean, the deck chair cushion turned over to hide the burn. The sky was a colorless scrim. A deer appeared in the yard, looking into the house, its eyes curious, almost expectant, but no one in the house had anything left to give.

A neighbor stopped…

Krystal Languell

(A neighbor stopped me (I was passing her store) (I was generally disgusted))

(She gestured to the street)   (and said   (You can't take all of this in))

((Make your mind like a piece of glass))

(I feel a deep moral debt)   (a suspicion towards joy)

(At the farmers market)   (my desire so appropriate)   (I allow myself to feel it)

(pure (abundance) of choice)   (a mouth full of luxury tomato with salt)

(Talking to death)   (advancing and clutching at)

(a stalk of Brussels sprouts (in conversation with) (sauerkraut in a jar))

((Here) food is cheap when raw (tonics for health))   (lavender sachets)

(The woman gave me licorice incense) (she said) (try this)

Surveillance

Stephen Haynie

The surveillance team settles into the city square unnoticed, or, if noticed, not noticed as a surveillance team.

In the Tuesday afternoon air there is the smell of spilt coffee and buttered popcorn. A film lets out. Men and women empty the theater and proceed west to cross the square, weaving among an equally large crowd just disembarking from the 218 bus heading west. Neither the filmgoers nor the cross-city travelers are of interest to the surveillance team. Perhaps, on a different day, they would be, but not this day. If this were the surveillance team's day off, or say a national holiday, they would not mind sitting back and observing with mild interest the people moving back and forth.

In the square a young boy fiddles with the string of a battered orange yo-yo while a group of seated teenagers take furtive drinks of bottles, flasks, cans, hiding the receptacles behind their backs whenever an overly-authoritative looking adult passes by. They snicker and jeer and give each other hi-fives. The boy is not of interest and the group of seated teenagers is not of interest.

Of interest is Paul Harrigan in grey slacks and a tweed sports coat, walking across the square, southerly, fixing the part in his hair with his fingers. Each member of the team takes note of Paul Harrigan's movements, but discreetly, which is something they have learned to do over many, many years. The surveillance team is interested in Paul Harrigan for two reasons: firstly, they are under his employ; secondly, they have found themselves inexorably involved in his situation, the situation for which they were hired three days ago, on an afternoon not unlike this one in the way in which the breeze blows like a muted trumpet in a black and white film and the trees sway like a slender woman slipping into a tight dress. The surveillance team is interested in how Paul Harrigan's situation will play out.

Paul Harrigan is still walking across the square, briskly self-aware, his left arm jaunty as it swings, his right hand in his pocket, likely thumbing a set of keys or, unwisely, a lighter. The surveillance team ponders over the potential accuracy of their assumption: really, Paul Harrigan could have most anything in that pocket, provided it fit. The surveillance team notes the impossibility of ever knowing what Paul Harrigan is thumbing in his pocket—if he is even thumbing anything at all.

The team is secreted throughout the square. The square has been infiltrated. Laughner is positioned in a tree as a performance artist, providing a solid vantage, while reciting lines from *Romeo and Juliet*. He is playing the part of Romeo. Square-walkers comment on the unconventional, though dramatically suggestive, positioning of Romeo speaking down to Juliet. Johnson is pushing an ice-cream cart along the perimeter of the square and making a profit. Heisner has an easel in front of him and is soliciting caricature sketches from passersby. Currently, he is working on a particularly comical sketch of an elderly couple. He exaggerates the angles and lines of their faces just enough to maximize humor and minimize insult. Miller sits on a park bench with a large stack of newspapers dating back seven months; the length of the surveillance is undetermined, and Miller prefers to be updated all at once. He starts with today's. The boy fiddling with the string of a battered yo-yo is actually Carlson, who is contracted, part-time, during the summer months, when his mother doesn't need him to run errands, and on select weekends. They are all wired with pieces in their ears and tiny microphones in their sleeves or clipped to the lapels of their jackets, depending on the style of the jacket.

Paul Harrigan has settled onto an empty bench. His right leg is crossed over his left, lifting and falling slightly to the tune played by a one-man band. Via a clever sequence of strings and levers, this man is able to manipulate, from what the team can gather, seven instruments: a guitar, a harmonica, two cymbals secured to the inside of his legs, bells on the tops of his boots, a large bass drum across his back which is struck by a felt-tipped mallet each time he clicks his right heel, a hi-hat positioned like a radio antennae over his left shoulder and which is struck each time he jerks down the neck of his guitar, and tied to his waist a thick rope which pulls behind him on a wheeled platform an effusive five-man jazz combo. This is a minor, though pleasurable, interest.

The surveillance team has been hired by Paul Harrigan to run surveillance on an expected encounter between him and one Linda, last name withheld. The encounter was organized six months ago, at the end of another previously planned encounter, in which Paul Harrigan and Linda, last name withheld, agreed to meet at this same square six months from that date.

Often they are not given all the details when working a job. They are told to follow this man, take pictures of this woman, and report back. Usually a client only provides the first name of the individual to be surveilled. In part this is to preserve anonymity; also, the omission of a last name suggests a less-complete, less-known person. The team prefers this withholding, their reason being that it mitigates the moral dilemmas inherent to their profession.

Occasionally, the team individually experiences moments of ethical guilt. It is an occupational hazard. This sensation, they determine, would be assuaged, if not completely eliminated, if the reason for the surveillance were stated. Of course they speculate. The lack of information stimulates the imagination and they inevitably find themselves placing these people within invented scenarios. Wealthy wives cheating on emotionally-distant husbands. Private accountants blackmailing powerful business executives.

At the end of the surveillance, though, they are expected to forget the whole thing and move on.

In this case, they have been instructed to tail Linda, the woman Paul Harrigan is expecting to meet. Paul Harrigan has not given a reason for the surveillance, only that they are to follow Linda from the square to wherever it is she goes.

The ideal outcome, Paul Harrigan said, is that you discover her place of residence. I want to know where she lives, he said.

A new line slowly forms outside the theater. Mothers keep their hands firmly attached to the shoulders of their children, who are struggling to free themselves, to rush into the theater, to break the display glass and gorge themselves on a variety of sugary confections.

The team has been given a photo of Linda. In the photo she is smiling at something off-camera (Laughner suggested a small child feeding pretzels to a curious squirrel, though Heisner asserted that it does not matter the cause of the smile, and that she isn't *smiling*, or in the *process* of smiling, but is in fact *finishing* a smile). Her hair is wavy and blonde and the team agrees that she looks much like a young Farrah Fawcett.

It is useful to note, Paul Harrigan informed the team, that Linda no longer looks like this, will definitely not look like this, and that the photo is, in fact, a photo of a young Farrah Fawcett. Explaining himself, Paul Harrigan explained that Linda will appear entirely differently than she ever has before.

She'll be wearing a disguise, the team said, relishing the intrigue.

No, Paul said, it isn't a disguise. She'll just look different. Imagine someone looking different from this photo.

Different in what way?

Every way. Imagine every way a person can look different. That's the way Linda will look.

The team nodded their heads, confused, and Miller pocketed the photo.

On the square Paul adjusts his legs, setting both feet on the ground. The team notes that, amazingly, Paul is doing nothing, is now not discernibly engaged in any physical action.

Beneath Laughner's tree a young child stretches out a pretzel to an inquisitive squirrel.

Over the radio Laughner contributes a metaphor: *Love is a small child feeding pretzels to a curious squirrel.*

Heisner counters the metaphor: *A small child feeding pretzels to a curious squirrel is a sinking lifeboat offering relief to a weary swimmer.*

This upsets Laughner, who rustles branches and shoos away tired birds.

A young woman is walking towards Paul Harrigan, who is still seated on the bench doing nothing. She does not look like a young Farrah Fawcett. The surveillance team perks up. Johnson ignores a braided girl's request for a Panther Pop, though after he collects her seventy-five cents. This could be her, they think. Paul Harrigan also suspects that the girl who looks nothing like a young Farrah Fawcett may be Linda. This is conveyed by the way in which Paul Harrigan slyly points at the woman, mouthing, This could be her. The woman notices Paul Harrigan's gesticulation, as small as it is, and slows her steps. She becomes aware that she is the focus of five additional sets of eyes, one up in a tree. She quickly turns left and exits the square. The braided girl sobs for her Panther Pop as Johnson pushes his cart towards Paul Harrigan.

Johnson asks Paul Harrigan if that was her. Paul Harrigan shakes his head, tells Johnson that he is certain that that young woman was not Linda. He speaks convincingly enough to Johnson.

Johnson asks if Paul Harrigan would like to buy an ice cream cone or Popsicle. Paul Harrigan declines. Johnson pushes his cart back into position, furious.

An afternoon open-air aerobics class assembles in the square. They lay out foam mats, stretch, and breathe deeply. A fit man sets down a twin-speaker stereo and presses play. The square is filled with music that excels in rhythm and repetition. The fit man leads the group in a series of lunges, twists, jumping jacks, and minor endurance exercises. It is healthy activity, designed to ease tension and loosen joints.

When the majority of one's waking hours are devoted to unearthing the secret life of another, it is difficult to maintain one's own sense of privacy. For this, the members of the team often find themselves disclosing personal information to each other. The disclosure is always unwarranted and without provocation.

Laughner speaks over the radio. He speaks of seeing his reflection in the shine of a Red Delicious apple at the grocery store four days ago. Gathering apples into his arms, he fell to his knees and wept.

The surveillance team, in the tedium of the surveillance, constructs narratives for Paul Harrigan and Linda, last name withheld. They do this to answer questions. How did Paul Harrigan and Linda first meet? Who initiated conversation? What was Linda's initial impression of Paul Harrigan? If Paul Harrigan were to recall memories of his dead father, would Linda also recall memories of her dead father? Was Paul Harrigan's father actually dead? Was Linda's father actually her father? If Paul Harrigan's father is actually dead, what was the cause of death? Was Linda's father/non-father involved in Paul Harrigan's father's death? Shouldn't he be? What were Paul Harrigan's father's final words to Paul Harrigan? What were Paul Harrigan's final words to his father? Does Paul Harrigan regret those final words and wish that he had said something more comforting, even if it was a lie? What reasons did Paul Harrigan have to lie to his father? What reasons did Linda's father have to lie about his paternity and involvement in Paul Harrigan's father's death?

These questions keep them occupied, though not satisfied, as they surveil the square, waiting for Linda.

After the afternoon open-air aerobics class clears out, a bouncing jumble of neon and Lycra, the square is empty for three whole minutes, excluding Paul Harrigan and the surveillance team. The magician appears, as if by magic, from an eruption of smoke directly in the center of the square. He raises his white-gloved hands and releases two doves into the air. They dive, twirl, and ascend, finally resting on a branch in Laughner's tree. He tolerates, and inwardly envies, their dove-ly display of affection.

The magician attempts to engage Paul Harrigan as he sits on the park bench. Paul Harrigan refuses to pick a card, any card. The magician resorts to finding objects within and around Paul Harrigan's body: a bouquet of flowers from his ear, a large gold coin from his nose, even produces a squirrel from one of Paul Harrigan's jacket pockets. The squirrel leaps from the magician's white gloves and looks around for a pretzel outstretched from the hand of a small child. This is of interest only to Laughner, who finds occasion to restate his previous metaphor. Laughner tires of the tree and the indigenous ants that crawl in his shirt collar and out his pant legs, biting judiciously. He also states that he has lost interest in the character of Romeo. Much of the ice cream in Johnson's cart has melted. Heisner is finishing a humorous and insulting sketch of an anthropomorphized pretzel feeding the likeness of Laughner to a distracted squirrel. Miller finishes the final newspaper, dated seven months ago. He folds the pages in silence, amazed. Carlson, hearing the shrill call of his mother, pockets the yo-yo and leaves without anyone noticing, resentful of his lack of involvement. They are waiting for something to happen, or for something to not happen, so that they are justified in ending the surveillance.

There is nothing of interest until the theater releases another crowd. A throng of children like salmon make their way across the square, their mothers, frustrated bears. The children, of all child-colors and child-sizes, run and skip and jump and climb over the square. They harass Johnson for ice cream. He tells them that it has all melted; they don't believe him, and he invites them to dip their hands in, which they do, to great amusement. They abscond with Miller's newspapers, sit under Laughner's tree, and make silly paper hats. They notice Laughner above them, vigorously scratching his itching thighs. They run, screaming, and alert their mothers, who rush the tree, righteously angry. Objects in their purses become projectiles as Laughner is pelted with lipsticks and compact mirrors. Heisner sketches the whole scene, rendering a faithful, naturalistic representation. He declares with noble resolve that he is through with caricatures. The children move from the surveillance team and the square like a colony of ants, streaming down side streets. Their mothers follow.

The square is silent again.

From the north end of the park walks a woman. She does not look like a young Farrah Fawcett. The surveillance team immediately takes note of her and declares her as something of interest. They speak into their sleeves or lapels.

Miller slips the photo out of his pocket and compares it to the woman. The photo is only a headshot, so he can only compare the woman's head to the head in the photo. The two heads look different. He tries to picture this woman looking away, smiling at a young child offering a pretzel to a curious squirrel.

This could be her, he says.

Laughner contributes a simile: *Anticipation is a woman walking across an empty square.*

Heisner gets up from his chair, walks to Laughner's tree, and shakes it mightily.

Still, the surveillance team is unsure if this is Linda, if the woman walking towards Paul Harrigan, seated, is the woman they have been hired to surveil.

Ultimately, they decide she is not Linda. She diverts her direction to Johnson and his ice cream cart. She gives him a dollar bill. Johnson pushes the cart to her, tells her to take it, which she does.

Again the surveillance team and Paul Harrigan are left alone on the square. Linda has not arrived, or did arrived, but left without making herself known. The team wonders: whose responsibility is it, then, to recognize Linda as Linda?

Over their radios the surveillance team discusses its options. Heisner suggests he calls his cousin, Sue, and asks her to come over and assume the role of Linda. She looks nothing like a young Farrah Fawcett, he tells them. The team considers this. They could throw in the towel, proclaim the endeavor a bust. They could take the earnings from the ice cream and the caricature sketches, get some kabobs at the Greek place owned by Johnson's neighbor, Mr. Papadopoulos.

However, each knows that they cannot leave until Linda appears. Their initial curiosity in whatever mutual history existed between Paul Harrigan and Linda had since mounted to an almost unbearable agony, likely compounded by the frequent periods of surveillance inactivity.

The 218 bus heading west reappears, this time bearing dozens of Japanese tourists who have come to tour the theater, which is, incidentally, somewhat of an historic monument. They set across the square. A long line forms in front of Heisner, and he hastily begins sketching. The tourists are disappointed with the realistic representations, likely preferring exaggerated images of themselves as George and Martha Washington, as the Statue of Liberty, as Hollywood actors. The tourists marvel at Laughner up in his tree as he half-heartedly recites Shakespeare, the crowd below shouting wherefore he art. They take turns photographing themselves sitting next to Miller, assuming he is a park vagrant by the unusual amount of old newspapers that surrounds him. Johnson, having sold the ice cream cart, is not of interest, and is passed by.

In the midst of the hustle and sudden interest in their covers, the surveillance team notices, distractedly, that Paul Harrigan has risen from the bench. He is looking over the heads of the tourists.

This is it, says Miller.

About time, says Johnson.

There, that's it, that's my last pencil, says Heisner.

What is it? asks Laughner. What is of interest?

The surveillance team feels that the end of their surveillance is near, that once they or Paul Harrigan identify Linda as Linda they will be able to move on, move away from the square, beyond the square, into everything that lies outside of the square.

Paul Harrigan slowly stretches out his arms as if to embrace someone. The surveillance team struggles to maintain focus over the clamor of the tourists. They are waiting for someone to step out from the crowd and into Paul Harrigan's open arms, or, at the very least, for someone to refuse the gesture. After surveilling for so long, they feel that they deserve at least that.

You, the Accused

Nicole Jost

CHARACTERS

YOU, Destiny. You are a twelve-year-old girl in the sixth grade.

MRS. JOY, the principal of your school. She's gigantic.

WHISPERS, quiet, grown-up voices you hear sometimes. The FIRST one has a scratchy voice like sandpaper. The SECOND one has a low voice, like if a bomb could be quiet. The THIRD one is sometimes nice, but sometimes not. . .

SETTING

Mrs. Joy's big, scary office. It's almost your last day of school! Outside it's hot, but not in here.

YOUR OUTFIT

Your outfit is really important to this story. You are wearing a purple tank top, purple platform sneakers that your mom just bought you, purple lipstick, and cutoff jean shorts.

SCENE

You've never been to the principal's office before.

This is a big room. Wow. This is a lot bigger than you would have thought. The walls must be one hundred feet tall.

MRS. JOY'S desk is so big you can't see the other side of it. It's shiny and dark, like hair on a shampoo commercial.

Even in your platform sneakers, you feel pretty small.

You've been waiting for a long time. The clock is ticking loud.
Then you hear them: the WHISPERS.

THIRD WHISPER

It's sort of a *cute* outfit. . .

FIRST WHISPER

A little *too* cute, if you know what I mean. . .

SECOND WHISPER

Who is she showing off for?

YOU

It's my favorite color.

ALL WHISPERS

Hmmm. . .

FIRST WHISPER

She has a boyfriend you know.

THIRD WHISPER

Oh dear.

SECOND WHISPER

Boy her age. Name of Sam.

YOU

We talk on the phone for hours. He walks me home.

FIRST WHISPER

Only twelve years old.

ALL WHISPERS

Tsk tsk tsk.

THIRD WHISPER

She's growing up too fast.

FIRST WHISPER

She even tried French kissing.

YOU

Tasted like spit.

SECOND WHISPER

Today French kissing, tomorrow God-knows-what.

THIRD WHISPER

She's a child! She should be doing childish things.

YOU

Like learning?

SECOND WHISPER

Wearing lipstick. And to school at that.

FIRST WHISPER

In my day, little girls were little girls.

ALL WHISPERS

Tsk tsk tsk.

THIRD WHISPER

She needs to be protected.

SECOND WHISPER

To be put in her place.

FIRST WHISPER

To be stopped before it's too late!

YOU hear big loud footsteps coming down the hall.

THIRD WHISPER

Someone's coming.

FIRST WHISPER

Finally!

SECOND WHISPER

Bout time someone put a stop to this.

YOU

I've never been called to Mrs. Joy's office before. . .

FIRST WHISPER

Won't be the last time.

SECOND WHISPER

Not for a girl like her.

*MRS. JOY walks through the door. She fits in her giant office, unlike you.
YOU feel even smaller. She smiles at you, but you can tell it's a lie.*

MRS. JOY

Okay, Destiny, let's have a little conversation. Would that be okay?

YOU

Yes, Mrs. Joy.

THIRD WHISPER

That's a good girl.

SECOND WHISPER

No use trying to fight it.

MRS. JOY

What you are wearing is not appropriate for school.

YOU

Oh. . .

MRS. JOY

All shorts must be fingertip length.

FIRST WHISPER

For modesty's sake!

THIRD WHISPER

And the preservation of childhood innocence in girls.

SECOND WHISPER

For God's sake, cover up.

YOU

But /

MRS. JOY

Do you understand?

YOU

But, I thought that was just for junior high school.

MRS. JOY

That's the rule.

YOU

But, I thought just for junior high school.

MRS. JOY

Stand up, please.

FIRST WHISPER

Take the test.

SECOND WHISPER

We'll be the judge.

YOU stand up.

MRS. JOY

Place your arms at your sides.

YOU do. Your fingertips touch the skin of your legs, instead of touching your shorts, which is the rule now.

ALL WHISPERS

Tsk tsk tsk.

MRS. JOY

You see? This is not appropriate for school.

YOU

I didn't know.

FIRST WHISPER

Now that's no excuse whatsoever.

THIRD WHISPER

Especially not for a smart girl.

SECOND WHISPER

What's the word her parents always called her?

ALL WHISPERS

Oh yeah: "Precocious."

YOU

I always wanted to be older.

FIRST WHISPER

It's cute to be ahead of the game

SECOND WHISPER

when you're six or seven

THIRD WHISPER

when you're preteen, it's

ALL WHISPERS

Dangerous.

MRS. JOY

I've brought you something to wear.

THIRD WHISPER

To keep you safe.

MRS. JOY pulls out the biggest, ugliest T-shirt in the whole entire world.

MRS. JOY

Put this on please.

YOU

But. . .

MRS. JOY

Young lady.

YOU

But, Mrs. Joy. . . it's too big.

MRS. JOY

Destiny, that's enough. Put the shirt on, please.

YOU put on the big, ugly T-shirt. It's so long, it looks like you aren't wearing any pants. You're embarrassed. The WHISPERS laugh at you. YOU pull on the shirt, to try to stretch it out. It doesn't help. The WHISPERS laugh louder and louder and louder.

SECOND WHISPER

Let the punishment fit the crime!

MRS. JOY

There. That wasn't so hard, was it?

YOU

It looks like. . .

MRS. JOY

Do you have something to say, young lady?

YOU don't even want to say it. . .

YOU

It looks like I don't have any pants on.

SECOND WHISPER

Well, that'll teach her!

THIRD WHISPER

Still, I *did* like how her lipstick matched her shoes. . .

FIRST WHISPER

She thought she was *so* cute, well,

ALL WHISPERS

look at her now.

MRS. JOY

Do you have something to say, young lady?

YOU

No, Mrs. Joy.

MRS. JOY hands YOU a tissue.

MRS. JOY

There is no makeup allowed in school.

YOU

I didn't know that.

MRS. JOY

Please remove your lipstick.

YOU do. YOU give her back the tissue. It's all smudged with purple, and some tears.

MRS. JOY

Destiny?

YOU

I'm. . . sorry Mrs. Joy.

SECOND WHISPER

Sorry for what?

THIRD WHISPER

For spoiling your schoolmates' fun?

FIRST WHISPER

Last year's sixth grade got to have a camping trip.

ALL WHISPERS

Not you.

FIRST WHISPER

They worried you would crawl into some boy's sleeping bag.

MRS. JOY

Do you understand why what you wore today was inappropriate?

YOU don't. Just that you're supposed to say you do.

YOU

Yes.

SECOND WHISPER

You think she'll change her wicked ways?

THIRD WHISPER

I hope so. . .

ALL WHISPERS

But I doubt it.

FIRST WHISPER

They all turn out this way nowadays.

MRS. JOY

I'm glad we had this talk.

YOU imagine that you're someplace else. Far away. Wearing your own shirt and not this big ugly one. Where MRS. JOY can't find you and the WHISPERS can't talk to you, and it's just quiet. YOU imagine someone nice to talk to.

YOU

This is how I like to be touched.

YOU touch your arm, very slow, very gentle. Like a tickle without the tickle.

End of play.

Cookies

Lindsay Hunter

At Bible study every week there were stale cookies all dumped on a platter like they fell from the sky, like God dropped them from his fist and there they landed on the plastic platter with the thin snowman etched in the center, its mouth a single round coal, or just a gouge into its snowhead, it was hard to say, but that snowman had a surprised look, like it was shocked it'd end up in the dollar bin at the drugstore after Christmas, shocked at the crack running through its middle like a scar, a scar you can't touch because it's on the inside, Miss Mabel said that's due to one of God's lesser favorites running it through the dishwasher despite her ending the Wednesday evening prayer with And please remind your flock to honor what we have by not putting cheap plastic items in the dishwasher and bless the children in Africa and China and wherever else Amen. The children all had a game where they ate the cookies as fast as they could and whoever ended up with the cookie that had been covering the snowman's face lost. Knowing you were about to uncover that shocked round face lent the same feeling as when you were about to be found during hide and seek: afraid you might pee, afraid you might scream, a whisper of rage. Every week Miss Mabel announced that there would be no more cookies the following week, yet every week there they were, leftovers from the gatherings between services on Sunday, a box of animal crackers someone forgot to close, sleeves of store brand Oreos softened from an unexpected rain, raspberry thumbprints forced on the pastor by a batty old lady who wouldn't take no for an answer. Some people need to contribute, Pastor Mike understands that, Miss Mabel said, in ways beyond those listed in the program every single week, I suppose. Some People was starting to feel as mysterious and real as the concept of God to the children. God was always watching you, but you were supposed to always be watching these Some People. Miss Mabel didn't used to be called Miss Mabel. Her name used to be Mrs. Richardson, a three-syllable last name that felt grand as a queen's to the children in her Bible study class, hard to imagine their Miss Mabel gliding around under a crown, Miss Mabel with her dry hands and hair that was oily at the top and tortured and fluffed where it hung at her shoulders and perfectly fine teeth but for a black spot that the children thought was a peppercorn or a piece of oregano from the spaghetti dinners, even a tiny chocolate chip until it became clear it was a permanent stain. No one had a three-syllable last name as far as the children knew. No King Richardson that they could find. And they had looked. Reports came in of someone's daddy saying Who? And another's momma saying Hmm now maybe and a different momma saying You just think about learning the word of the Lord and not stomping around in trash, the children confused on that one for a while until someone suggested the trash wasn't real trash but the trash of gossip. Which meant there was trash to be had. Miss Mabel had no ring but the children felt sure there used to be a ring, you could see its absence in the shiny ring-shaped indent circling her finger. A scar that wasn't a scar, like the snowman's dishwasher injury. There will be no cookies next week, Miss Mabel said again, but the cookies came, someone had overbought for a child's classroom birthday party, the good kind, the kind that stayed soft no matter how long they sat open, the kind that filmed your teeth and tongue long after you'd finished chewing. The children wondered just who in the congregation had the kind of riches to overbuy the good kind of cookies and then discard them at the church like any old common Nilla, they were starting to think like Miss Mabel, someone who had been a queen and was now a common Nilla. Mrs. Richardson, the children hissed, too quiet and quick for Miss Mabel to pick it up, but she looked up from the devotional she was reading, her eyes darting, trying to catch it, but the children didn't dare. What God means here, Miss Mabel said, is that it's okay to fail, as long as you're not an idiot about it. God didn't use the word idiot because that is a newer word but that is the gist. Mrs. Richardson, a daddy reportedly said, I forgot all about that she was married, but didn't go on. The cookies were offered at gatherings between services, then to the men who came for Men's Group on Sunday night, then to adult Bible study on Mondays, and finally to the children on Wednesdays. They had made the rounds, been passed over, this was their last shot at glory, and the children began to feel responsible for bringing the life cycle of each cookie full circle. Getting each down in two bites or less was key, and avoiding the snowman's face was even more important. The Holy Trinity was God, Some People, and Miss Mabel, each one unknowable to the children, who at bedtime, in the dark, worried for the snowman's loneliness, worried the snowman needed a purpose, and so prayed for the cookies. The children couldn't say what would happen if too many were three-biters, or if you had an evening where you had a three-biter and you uncovered the snowman's face. They couldn't put it into words but it felt like the combination could turn you from a queen to a Miss Mabel. Could make your kingdom expel you, forget all about you shut up in the Bible study room with its busted wicker rocker and mismatched folding chairs and the stain that seemed to creep and grow up the striped wallpaper and the dead refrigerator that doubled as a toy box and a lost and found and the picnic table where you had to set the church's worst platter down to present the cookies no one else in the entire congregation wanted to eat, and where the children looked at you with crumbs on their lips and collars, waiting for you to explain what God means by it all.

Advice from Stevie Nicks on Dreaming

Tyler Kline

Think bluegrass: how to disappear a man feet first or discover
    no body at all. Foxglove: what kills before nightfall

growing silent as the razor, the leather & denim shoreside pulling rain.
    If you are thinking fever, there will be no sleep:

your limbs tire restless as piano wire in a woman's hands. Until
    someone goes missing there is still night & these are your lips

humming the diner full: people you have stored in the car blocks
    of your mind—missing dog collars, cassette tapes, shadowboxes.

A handbreadth from the door, a man pouring coffee like the flicker
    of a motel sign. Think: until a country sweats there is still burning,

a woman beginning to light the pyre with her hands.
    Do not think headlights, motor oil, because behind that jukebox

there is always another song, a voice tallying the doves your mind
    has just freed from the pie display, counting too, the ones

flocking to the field. Go ahead, guess. How many until the corn—
    ready to be shucked—is mistaken for your ghost.

10 Questions for John Berryman

Kevin A. Phan

What fell out of your life first,
    Henry or your hairline?
Are you joking holy loudness
    from beyond tomb?
Or are you ghostface,
    blooming within hells?
How much sunlight died
    in the naked frenzy of your beard?
Were you constantly shedding tears
    to grow the rainbows?
Were you the drunk weatherman
    predicting future storms?
Did you run naked through storms
    among snapping trees
    laughing & howling?
Is your stripper name
    Black Organic Honeybear?
Is Mr. Bones a tumor
    within our culture-rainbow
    bleeding under the American dream?
Is your afterlife, Sir, a snowing
    of foam erasing
    —endlessly
    —forever?

Dementia

Michael Trocchia

". . . it is not clear that clemency *[clementia]* ever assumed a meaning distinct from that of a host of near-synonymous terms, including *misericordia, lenitas, humanitas, mansuetudo, liberalitas, comitas, modestia, temperantia, magnitudo animi, modus,* and *moderatio,* along with the verbs for sparing and forgiving. . ."

—from David Konstan's "Clemency as a Virtue"

His daughter, visiting again, was digging
up bulbs in the garden. He was inside,
sleeping in his chair, his mouth open.
So when the thief came in and saw him
there, he took the words right out of his mouth—
one word after another, as if on the string
of a child's kite. No, you say, it was not quite
like that: the words came out more like
handkerchiefs of an old magician, knotted
together at the ends. And who could argue
with you? For, yes, when his daughter found
the thief, he was caught in the thornbush,
spitting up meanings for the dove, while
her father, dozing through it all, dreamed
of feathers caught in the air, just before
the winds, he would say, let them go.

MAY CAUSE
SYMPTOMS OF
...MILD DEPRESSION
ANXIETY
NAUSEA
INSOMNIA
DIARRHEA
AND / OR
CONSTIPATION...

I'VE BEEN
A MINER
FOR A
HEART OF GOLD

EYES
ARE
PRODUCTIVE
AND
SELFISH
DREAMING
MACHINES

WEEKEND TAG SALE . . .

HEY BLUE
HERE IS A SONG
FOR YOU
INK ON A PIN

WHY BUY A MATTRESS ANYWHERE ELSE?

HALF OF WHAT
I SAY IS
MEANINGLESS
JUUUUULIAN

SOME
KIND
OF
FAMILIAR
SHADOW
. . .
SOME
NEW
PRESENC
IN MY
PRESENCE
STAY
TUNED
FOR 30 MINUTES
OF HITS! COMIN
UP

Barry 71

WAIT.
HOW DID I ·GET HERE?
CALLING SISTER MIDNIGHT

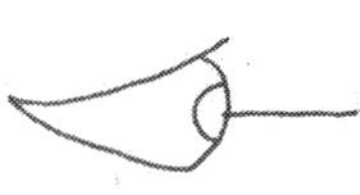

THESE
DAYS

The Mother Totem

Michael Mungiello

Although the Mother totem is inanimate ninety-nine percent of the time, it does do one animate thing. The Mother totem expresses regret.

At the bottom of the Grand Canyon back before it was the Grand Canyon back when it was underwater back when everything was underwater, was where the Mother totem was first found. Fish intuited the implications thereof and avoided the area around it for centuries.

The Mother totem invariably compels its possessor to begin weeping and organizing his receipts for tax purposes. The Mother-in-Law totem does not exist. This is a myth I am happy to dispel.

The Mother totem derives joy from company, in its inanimate way; it also regards company as inevitable. I, on the other hand, on both counts. . .

Once the Mother totem and I went to see *Mamma Mia* at our local AMC. I assumed it enjoyed the film, for it did not express regret.

A brief clarification: the only thing the Mother totem expresses is regret. Everything else it *feels* finds its expression *through you*. Hence your "inexplicable" diarrhea, headaches, stomach cramps, depressions, intoxicating fantasies, and vivid impressions of betrayal.

I dream of sea walruses waltzing through Atlantic City casinos. I awake to find I have been robbed and the Mother totem is gone.

My first impulse is to consult the Father totem, but then I remember that the Father totem, like the Mother-in-Law totem, is just a myth, one of the Mother totem's many fantasies. My second impulse is to buy a new Mother totem from the jeweler's on West 53rd. This is a significantly more feasible option.

Memories of my Mother totem flit through my troubled dreams. Here we are eating ice cream on the Wildwood boardwalk:

Here we are crying in my backyard after my pet turtle died:

Here we are at my first wedding, and my first divorce:

I awake in a sweat with a bloody nose, my yellow teeth staining red.

It will take me a month to save up enough money to buy another Mother totem. Stolen, it must be expressing regret. But I wouldn't know now. Every other time it has expressed regret, I've been there. I've never not been next to it.

What does the Mother totem's expression of regret sound like? Flickering fluorescent lights, cigarettes stubbed out in the snow, the sputtering of a car engine, clothes sliding down a laundry chute, a dripping faucet, the whimpering of a dog who is so old she can no longer climb the stairs to her owners' bedrooms, the unoiled wheels of an uncooperative shopping cart, rusty hinges, heart palpitations. . .

Johanna raps at my door with her bediamondringed knuckles. She sports a burgundy cloak and black John Lennon-style sunglasses. This I can see from my peephole. Out of sight until I've welcomed her in and sat her down on my couch and initiated intense lovemaking are her large bronze hoop earrings, which she takes off and later puts back on. Whether it was I or the Mother totem who orgasmed, I cannot say.

The following morning, over Louisiana Crunch Cake and coffee beige with cream, my ex-wife implores me to not proceed with my planned purchase. I pour the remainder of my coffee onto the potted miniature cactus in the middle of my kitchen table. "What if it is expressing regret even now," she says.

But, I think to myself, once Johanna's gone to the airport, maybe this thief had his Mother totem stolen in turn. Perhaps in time I will steal someone else's.

But I am getting used to living without my Mother totem: the late-night television, the white-collar crime, the adulterous affairs with diplomats' wives, and the nocturnal nudist beach excursions I've begun embarking on. . .

(Jalopies honk in the street below. Each has a bumper sticker reading, "Honk if the claims of psychoanalysis are outmoded and patriarchal." They are going to an all-night Jalopy party.)

But when I do sleep, when I am not buck-naked or boning, my dreams are increasingly terrible. New memories, of my Mother totem happy with the kidnapper; of the thief introducing it to his children and their Mother totems; of my Mother totem placed at a lavish Thanksgiving dinner, expressing no regret, watching *I Love Lucy* from the lap of the kidnapper, expressing no regret, and at night on the pillow beside the thief who has now installed thief-proof locks on his windows and doors. . .

I call Johanna on her work phone. "I can't talk right now. We're about to board." I tell her I'll need help rescuing my Mother totem. "I can't," she says. "I'm on back-to-back redeyes from Mali to Oregon to Tibet to Hong Kong to Egypt to Rome," and so on, "but I should be back by the end of the month." The doorbell rings. Somebody has sent me three dozen roses, with three dyed blue. The card is signed, "Somebody."

The Mother totem functions optimally when in propinquity to roses.

I mull over the roses' significance.

I read in a promotional email that the jeweler's on West 53rd is running out of Mother totems. There has been an increase in demand and, due to deforestation, overfishing, and the death of the bees, a decrease in supply.

Now I dream I am swimming with manatees through the ruins of Phoenician banks, replete with pre-modern ATMs and fishbowls full of lollipops carefully sealed in translucent green plastic. I wake up gasping, of course, but also sort of chortling, sinisterly. Johanna returns the day after tomorrow, a few hours after my paycheck will clear (direct deposit).

An uneventful day passes. An uneventful night ensues.

I look up how much it would cost to fly from Mali to Oregon to Tibet to Hong Kong to Egypt to Rome. It's about as much as a new Mother totem.

I wake up and feel nothing and shower quickly and eat only half of my blueberry scone. I play Mahler's 9th symphony as conducted by Karajan and feel nothing. I play the same as conducted by Bernstein and still feel nothing. By this time it is only eight and I'm not expected in the office for another hour and a half. I know that if I go to work I will continue feeling nothing so I email my boss, telling him I have come down with something.

I answer my vibrating phone. "Listen, Johanna—" But it's not her. "Listen, Boss—" But it's not him either. Instead, the voice of a crotchety old man. "Fuckwad!" He croaks. "Mooncalf! Scoundrel! Rattlepate! Half-wit! Loser! Gudgeon! Saphead!" He continues even after I put the phone down. I turn the volume all the way up. From the couch I can hear little rustlings of thin pages in a big book under his filthy mouth. It goes on from afternoon to evening. Several times Johanna tries calling but I decline.

I wake up still on the couch. There's a note on the coffeetable, recommending a Window Repairman, suggesting that I will receive a significant discount if I mention that I know "Rich the Thief."

Beneath that note is another note, which reads, "Also the Mother totem asked me to forward you this message." The message is this:

I forward my wilting roses (I have neglected to put them in water) to Johanna, who is probably off on her next flight. She's not in town for more than one day usually, which was maybe half of the reason we got a divorce.

I sit frozen as a corpse for three days and nights, as empty as an airship museum.

I would like to imagine the expression of my regret sounds like books burning, salmon gasping in the mouths of brown bears, granite melting onto magnolias, overheated pelicans plummeting into the Atlantic, wedding bells tolling, clapping at the conclusion of an auction. . .

Melanie Sleeping

Anna Rotty
2016, PHOTO INK ON PAPER

Woven

Ashley Johnson
DIGITAL PHOTOGRAPH, ACRYLIC YARN POM, MAGNOLIA BLOSSOMS

Nighttime Feed

Mia Ayumi Malhotra

The soft gurgle of milk as it tumbles
down your throat, the *suck-suck-swallow*
I've learned to listen for in this elbow-
joint of night, hour of waking sleep,
when all I see is your forehead's gleam,
the bright bridge of your nose. Light
leaks in from the windows. Eyes closed,
lashes two dark smudges, you feed
as if in a dream, our sleep-soaked bodies
somehow having found each other.
No clock ticking, no traffic noise,
just the rhythmic tug of your palate.
You, me. Cradled in the crook of sleep,
you grunt, and your tiny arm curls
around my side. Your warm body—
how solid you've grown, all the creases
filled in—is it possible it remembers?
Pressed against my belly—that dark hold—
do you remember the half-lit home
we made together? All those months,
your fluttering form, the turns you took.
Limb bud, spinal column. When exactly
did your soul split from mine, pinched
like a bud from its branch? You stir, then still,
cheek pressed against my breast. I marvel
at the perfect spiral of your ear, damp
hair curled around the lobe where you've
worked it with sticky fingers. Your fist
clenches, releases. Our orbiting bodies,
for the moment at rest, two familiar planets
making their way through the night.

Big-Headed Anna and the Blue Virgin

Stephanie Dickinson

Ciudad Juárez. 1917.
Big-Headed Anna and the Baby Thieves
From Black Bayou to the Rio Grande

Black Bayou. 1916. I'm afraid of the night hunter—owls picking off mice and feral cats. I hear their cries and caterwauling as they are taken up and emptied of life. I have never had a friend. My baby will be my first. The sun sets and she wakes with the most heartrending shriek, followed by her hum, a kind of birdcall. Birds singing like they do straight through rain and thunder call to her and she tries to answer. Slowly, it grows pitch black except for sparking fireflies and misty yellow clots. In the darkness the souls glow; they're always here but without moonlight they shine, they carry what the slaves made their light with. I can see burning scarves bobbing in the water. Light from grease lamps, an iron bowl filled with lard and a rag floating in it for flame. A long time ago a magnolia tree grew here and the blossoms opened. The scent is still so strong. A white room you can walk into and be gone. Mosquitoes want to live in my hair, and in my **leaf-colored eyes.** I grab the oars and row to the middle where no one will pester us. I don't remember picking my baby up, but she's in my arms and I press my nose to her head, inhaling the whiteness. Her suck is strong. I've never felt anything like this. If I had been standing I would have fallen. I could feel it leaving my body, all the shiners and croakers, all the summer nights when I slept in the heat, all the milking of cows, the ladling of soap, all the everything flowing out of me into this hunger. My infant is soft as an egret nest and I hold all her warmth against my chest. Around me water skimmers breed and spiders hunt with their nets, dragonflies court in mid-air, mites cling to hosts, a crawfish digests its old shell. Words catch on my teeth. *I love you.* There's just the two of us listening but that's enough. I offer myself to be eaten.

Ciudad Juárez. 1916. Before I crossed the Rio Grande half of me had already vanished. My hands were a mess of cow pox, my lips welted with horsefly bites. I was that big-headed girl in the bait house trying to nurse her baby girl. People said I was slow-witted and couldn't raise a wee one. The baby snatcher who stole her took her to a rich gringo in Monterrey. And there was all the milk that my baby would have drunk, making my chest swell and my nipples crack, until I had to squeeze out the watery gruel. When I stood over the trough with a jelly jar of human milk, I tried some. It tasted sweet. I was drawn to Mexico's yawning nostrils and ocher wind crying, *"Death to the Wealthy."* I wasn't afraid of rebels torching factories. I knew the rich had sent out buyers to find infants, men strong as horses who ate their stew in a street cafe manned by women missing fingers. When I came for my beans, I'd see a nick or a scar on a hand, and I wanted to ask how it happened. Thin girls frying tortillas in the bread line looked famished, their eyes black suns, their stomachs rumbling with jaguar hunger. Sometimes when I reached for corn bread I would try to touch their hand, but they always drew far away, as though it was the deer of the moon I was trying to comfort. *I'm not bad—you can see that, can't yo*u? I buy the day-old bread. I keep one eye watching my shoulder—my great-aunt with her singed arms from a burnout, her eyes of blue stones, lashes like glass splinters. Provincial, she is all things gnashing and flowing with lava, she, the seller of my daughter, all things chaotic. Pancho Villa's cast shadow knows her. From the bodies in the graves stubbed out or left cut into pieces by *Federales*, ghosts pick up the pole-axe, hammer, and puntilla. They stab until the mahogany earth bleeds, slowly. The deep dirt is bone. I keep following the milk scent of my baby through this land where guts nailed to trees are told to walk.

Chihuahua. 1918.

Big Headed Anna Arrested
for Vagrancy

Chihuahua. 1918. No sun penetrates the deep stone. Stairs funnel up towards a cell, the rusty key squeaks open. I am pushed inside. My hands find the bunk that sags with the weight of someone lying there. *Cabezóna Loca*, she sniggers, who put you here? Her fingers strike a blue sulfur match. They stole your money, basket-head, and then said you were a vagrant. You sleep on the floor. I am a rebel. *Las soldaderas.* I can call her Zorro, the fox. What is inside that big-head of yours? she laughs. Stupidity? The Fox tells me she no longer hopes to return as a jaguar, the dead god reborn. After her execution she'll hunt the vile Cortes into the afterlife. Here, you look hungry. She shares the goat chorizo and tortilla smuggled to her by the child with the withered arm. Zorro traces a mole on her upper lip, a scar across her cheek as though the claw mark made—the last act of a rooster in the jaws of the she-fox. Hair unraveling as if rope, she plaits and unplaits. I fought in the revolution for the peasants, she tells me. I killed. How many? Many. She orders me to listen, to picture the man's head, held firmly between her elbow and torso, see his lip and chin sweating. Sometimes she wedged the mouth open with a doorknob. I raised the pole axe at the base of the skull, one quick motion. The slipper-orchid of blood still blooms in my sleep since the scorned men did not go easily. I'll adorn myself in fragrant Belly-of-the-Night hyacinth. The guards will eat chili peppers at the firing squad's rifles. I wanted for nothing growing up, a stucco house, a courtyard, fiddlewood trees in a grove. I can see my mother and stepfather behind their high gates. My mother is beautiful. Look at how she lies on the bed. Red lips unsmiling. Her throat is cut and she tries to hold it together. The sheets glisten with passion fruit's tiny seeds. My stepfather's thumb is severed and some *Federal* stuffed it into his mouth. Here, big-headed girl, take my hand, hold it. They'll come for me in the morning, their eyes no longer burning but cinders of eaten stars.

Mexico City. 1919.

Big-Headed Anna Eating Fire at
the Plaza Del Ángel

Mexico City. 1919. I cut pictures out of Holy Day calendars in honor of the brown Madonna, able to withstand unquenchable scorching, who appears to her followers wearing a gun belt. A Zapatista. I followed my feet down the riverbank into the swimming city of the fish. Our Lady of Guadalupe joined me in the current, like the Jesus Lizard she could walk on water. How can I live, mother, I have no one. I am told there is work in the slaughterhouses. The Madonna caresses the innocent girls who hold knives, although not liking what they do. To stab the horses and hear the last whinny. To gaze into the amber eyes of butchered light. To smell the saliva of grass. Then the dismembering—turds hard as emeralds, the hunger in its guts, intestines painted in shit and blood. We horse-stabbing girls stroll between the donkey carts and wagons, selling tortillas and shreds of mare meat. I try being one of the horse-girls, but I can no more run the withered stallion through with a knife then amputate my own hand. I set him free. How can I live; I have no one. She shows me how to drink flames. How to exhale plumes of fire. Come hither, camels, who once roamed the Valley of Mexico. Tailbone and coccyx. Hoof. Ventricle. Gall bladder. I pour the raw fuel between my lips. "Drink. That is my body," says the brontosaurus, "a million years have I fermented." Yes, nods the asteroid of 1.5 billion years ago who sucked a third of molten Mexico into space where it froze. I strike the match. The Lady loves me; she won't allow my tongue to turn green or my gums to blacken. Sightseers fill my begging tin. I gulp down more fuel. Breathe out a peacock's tail of red fanning halos of blue. When I swallow fire, I become a purring cat, a long purple dress; I hold burning between my lips—at 120 degrees snow is falling, and I walk before it goes dark inside me. I am a spindly tree, a high ceiling, the moon, blue and huge as a fat rabbit, a platter, and the trail my bare feet drag cocooned in ice. *I will smite every horse with astonishment,* says Zechariah 12:1-3. *I will smite his rider with madness. Like a torch of fire in a sheath.* My dreams are pale tangerine or lemon depending on how the sun shines.

Insurgencia

Laura Cesarco Eglin

Me creció un pomelo
en el estómago, hace ya
unos días que decide
en qué dirección abrirá
los gajos, los tejidos que
van a rasgarse, los que se van
a acomodar. Y no tengo
que hacer nada de eso.
Un pomelo entiende y yo
no irrumpo. Esto es un capítulo
aparte de la digestión. Si observo bien
adentro, cada bolsita de jugo—
la poética de lo amargo tiene color
amarillo. Invita a hacerme de
filamentos, agasajar así
al pomelo, escucharlo.

Mutiny

translation by
Jesse Lee Kercheval & Catherine Jagoe

A grapefruit has grown
in my stomach; it's been
deciding for some days
which way it will open
out in segments, which tissues
will be torn, which
rearranged. I don't
have to do anything.
A grapefruit understands and I
won't interrupt. This is separate
from the chapter on digestion. If I look hard
inside, every bit of juice—
the poetics of bitterness is
yellow. It invites me to become
filaments, to welcome
the grapefruit, listen to it.

All Love Is Good Love

Emily Kendal Frey

When I think about food

My bones crinkle in

Mounds of white sand

A wet desert

Lemon custard, light yellow

Hold it close to your etheric body

Everyone was made

In a similar moment

My dad moves around his house

It gets dark

There's skin with a texture

On the back of his neck

I didn't believe

I could go beyond thinking

Joy a pill in the cupboard

Dole it out

Night is scary because we can't see it

But even when the sun was out

We failed to notice

And now it's morning again

And all the evil you were while asleep

Demonstrates itself across your face

At the doctor's office

I grew a set of wings

It's not what I would have chosen

But all love is good love

Then I went into the next

Part of my life

Not less

But not more

Shortcuts

Glenn Kinen

There is nothing worse than being broke and fat. The keywords of my girlhood. I can dredge up other adjectives if you want—insecure, academic, bored—but broke and fat are what woke me up in the morning and lay me to bed at night. I didn't live in a cardboard box, and I didn't weigh four hundred pounds—that, at least, would have had a certain glory. No, I was age fifteen, weight 220, height 5'2", and my sole salary was unspent lunch money. I grew up in South Miami, by Delgado Second-Hand Plaza, a baby blue strip mall that housed a dozen thrift stores, lined up like mug shots. Books—a Harvard Classic, a sex manual—cost a nickel, while a chandelier or a cherub set you back ten bucks. Even in Goodwill, guys have it better: they can walk out with a dead man's suit and look like the world. A woman pulls a blouse off the rack, and it's zebra print with shoulder pads. Or a babushka overcoat. Polyester hot pants. A dirndl. I'd strip in the aisle, trying dress after dress, watching out for passersby, naked, clothed, naked, the rejects falling to a pile, until I'd found a polka dot tunic that nearly fit.

I say broke and fat because you can't speak Spanish. *Una gorda sin dinero,* that's what I heard, my ear pressed against the inside of the front door, listening to my father and his friend Raimundo bullshit on the porch. Raimundo came by every Saturday morning, bearing a shopping bag filled with Budweiser and cheese, and they'd sit in those plastic chairs until dusk. He had a thin gray moustache, and always wore a white linen jacket, a pink azalea hanging off his lapel. He looked like the pimp of all Havana, out slumming with my father. He celebrated New Year's by shooting his revolver into the air, aiming right at the moon. But the main thing was that he was old, born forty years before my dad, and he talked the worst shit. These old, black Jehova's Witnesses used to make their rounds once a month, sweating in their suits, and Raimundo would chant *monos, monos,* raising his voice when one of them stared his way. If a mother walked by with her son, he'd yell at the son: "You keep thinking of fucking her, Jesus will send you to hell!"

You asked me if I had sex in adolescence. All I wanted. You asked me if I had friends. Plenty. I snuck into raves in Fort Lauderdale, the crowd dancing until dawn, a thousand dilated pupils staring at the sun. School? I won the science fair, the haiku contest. Oh, I got so skinny later, and I've stayed so skinny since. And you, my sesquipedalian, could never leave me at thin; you called me wispy, svelte, gamine, your sylph, your willow, and I taught you *flaca,* too. But back then, before you, I despised my jiggling arms, my girl gut. I loathed my reflection. The worst part of being fat isn't even the bloated flesh. It's the shrunken soul. I wanted to joke, to snicker, to talk trash, to share that joy of contempt, and I couldn't. You can be as clever as you want, but a fat girl's a fat girl and that's that.

My hook-up at the pharmacy wanted two hundred to swipe a bottle of diet pills. I started saving quarters in a pickle jar, but in two months I only had forty dollars. I've done jumping jacks: there's more dignity in amphetamines. I'd schemed for work—waitress, papergirl— when opportunity found me. Raimundo drove home one Saturday, three-quarters drunk, and his eighty-two-year-old heart stopped like a sentence. His last rite was to swerve left, tumble over the median, and block both lanes of traffic.

Raimundo had a son, a chiropractor, and he ran the details. Sold Raimundo's car for scrap. Canceled his catalogs. Cremated him. My father drove Raimundo south, his brass urn sitting shotgun, the chiropractor in the back. You pass dozens of islands on the way to Key West, drive on the Seven Mile Bridge. And at end, you reach a stone monolith, painted black and red: "90 Miles to Cuba." The chiropractor took the urn, cradling it like a baby or a cat, and kissed the monolith. Then he held the urn straight up, gripping it with the tips of his fingers, and he walked into the sea, in shoes and slacks, walking until the water was at his neck, and the chiropractor stopped, scattering his father into the ocean, as close to Cuba as he could get him.

The next day, 6:00pm, a phone call. The chiropractor again. He needed to get rid of Raimundo's house, and offered my father seven hundred to clean it out. My dad shook his head, whispered a can't-do-no-thank-you, and hung up the phone. He leaned into his recliner hard so his legs kicked up in a snap, and he turned on *Jeopardy*. He clicked up the volume so that the contestants were screaming, "Where is purgatory? What is amnesia? Who was Pavlov's dog?"

I asked, "What are you doing?" I yelled, "WHAT ARE YOU DOING?" He turned the volume up still more, to sixty, to sixty-five, and how could he hear me through all that? I shut off the TV.

"I was watching that," he said, staring at the ceiling. Popcorn stucco, with a puff of silver dots. When I was seven, I sat on his shoulders and tossed glitter into the drying plaster.

"Who called?"

"Wrong number."

"I was listening on the line."

"We're doing just fine," he said. My dad was thin as a post, and was sunk into the green velour of our thrift-store recliner.

"Look at me," I told him.

His eyes were fixed on the glitter.

What were my options? A thousand hours of running? Vomiting after dinner? Life is about shortcuts.

I put my face inches in front of his.

"Look at me," I repeated.

His eyes tilted down, scanning the floor.

"We'll split the work," I said.

"We?"

"And the money."

"What are you going to do with three-fifty?"

"A girl needs cash."

We left the next day, me and my dad both wearing Miami Dolphins sweats, driving down I-95 at 7:00am. The sun was orange and looked like it took up half the sky. It's an illusion—objects grow on the horizon—but it didn't look like an illusion. Whatever glamour Miami has, the coconuts and salsa, stays hidden on the highway. A million Cubans in Florida, and rednecks own all the billboards: every sign from Miramar to Kendall is for barbeque or go-karts or waterbeds. Remember when you told me we are all sinners? I said, Not you.

My dad talked the whole ride down: boyhood friends who died, the danger of car travel. I was listening, but I wasn't. I dreamt of myself after the pills: skinny, bitchy, a boy-killer—and what I could buy with the money left over—SAT books, leather journals, ballet flats, a pipe, tattoos. He told me that time accelerates as you grow older. My mind ran rings around bracelets, silver crucifixes, Greyhound tickets, onyx studs, gin, Converse, a belly-button ring. My teeth bit into my lower lip.

You are sighing: why does she write this to me? You once said I must know your fracture, and now you must know mine.

Raimundo's house was one story tall, with crew-cut hedges, bookended by mango trees. The lawn was a perfect rectangle. A plastic flamingo guarded a bush of azaleas. His house was painted peach. My father put in the spare key and nodded. To open a door is an act of faith.

Listen. It smelled like a sewer. Like a cow exploded. I knocked over a glass jar and a burp of yellow foam spilled out over the shards. The living room was stocked with trash. Egg shells, sandwich bags, oil filters, VHS tapes, candelabras, handles of whiskey, parts of a tire, dented cans, pork rinds, dirty sleeping bags, rotting beets, rope, pillows, feathers, a book about mummies, wet cardboard, onion skins, snotted handkerchiefs— each is a thing now, but then it was trash. Trash to the ceiling. Trash in piles. Trash in clumps. Trash in towers. Forts of trash. Trash ramparts. Say a room is a box. Two thirds of that box was trash.

It was the most impressive thing I'd ever seen.

My father gazed into space like he had two glass eyes, his mind bobbing for two minutes. Then he pouted, a tiny exhalation, a pursing of the lips. "We shouldn't be here," he said.

"Let's take a wide front," I said. "Or maybe make a narrow path. Do you want to work together or split it up?"

He stared past me, his gaze diffuse, the sun burning into the black of his pupils and reflecting back at me—a bright, tiny dot.

"You know, Mr. Harris at school always says the way to get started is to start."

I flashed an Honor Roll smile, but he just pushed out a few slow words, half-speech, half-groan: "He was my friend. You don't know. You're a little girl."

"I'm not a little girl."

He turned around, his back to the trash, looking out the door. His truck had a full tank of gas. My pockets were empty.

There are two kinds of diet pills. One blocks absorption. Pizza, sausage, oatmeal—all pass right through: you turn into a tube. The other is an appetite suppressant, an amphetamine, speed. But calling them diet pills is an understatement: they make you better at everything. Diet pills moved my sofas. The hiked me up the Appalachian Trail. They read the Gospels to me. They wrote you letters in longhand—what did you call them, my missives? Those missives, where I moaned about my work, or my men, or where you indulged me as I played poetess, or where you heard a woman confess that you were handsome, or more than handsome—those missives—the ones that sit in your leather box, that you've read ten dozen times—those were written by diet pills.

Here was the plan. We'd dig out a path starting from the front door, through the living room, hitting the kitchen, and running down the hall into what I figured was the bedroom. It'd begin as a thin trail, but as we hauled out garbage, the road would widen, like lanes being added to a highway. I gave my father the Dollar General gloves, our only pair, and brought in the aluminum garbage can. I'd fill the can; my dad would unload it into the dumpster.

It took six hauls to clear our first patch of land. The trash sat in layers. The crust was dead receipts, magazines, junk mail, coupons. The mantle was a tangle of coaxial cable and power strips—and the core was a barbecue. A tiny Weber grill. The lid creaked as I opened it. Spoiled chicken, drumsticks bruised purple, smelling like a prison toilet. I nearly threw up, but squelched it down. I tried fitting the grill into a garbage bag, but the top half fell off: charcoal hit the ground and puffed into dust. I wiped sweat and ash from my forehead.

"Did you know he was a pig?" I asked.

"Claudia, please."

"Did you?"

"He's gone."

"This is a sty. He breathed this."

"Gone."

"In and out. This was his air."

"You wanted to be here," he said.

"Why didn't you know?"

"People aren't how they look."

Remember when I moved into your studio? I saw your eyes groan. Your apartment was edited, cleansed, and my little suitcase unloaded its chaos of novels and bras. You tried to laugh, but even then, with a rainbow of underwear on your floor, you were earnest, all demons and aspirations.

I stood in my clear little patch. The house was hot, aching with that Miami heat that is deep and damp and leaves you stupid. The sun shone, illuminating this junkyard like a movie set. I had a path to cut. From here to the bedroom. I pulled the trashcan behind me. I closed my eyes. Jack Kerouac wrote *On the Road* on diet pills, not even on single pages, but on a paper taped together, a long scroll fed into a borrowed typewriter, a missive to everyone.

My arms hurt. My thighs stuck together. My bra was wet. I panted. My father threw an alarm clock through the window to let in air and patted my shoulder. I opened a black felt box, and a swarm of rosaries fell out. My father helped me toss an oscilloscope. *National Geographics*. Paper dolls of Abraham and Mary Lincoln. We'd only cleared two feet of trail. I prayed for a prize. But no emeralds, no gold jangles, no daggers with swastika handles. I was a fat girl in the town dump. Next came Raimundo's bird cages, twenty of them, made of rusted wires and filling up the next stretch of trail. There were no birds, no skeletons of birds, no newspaper lining. They imprisoned tchotchkes, bric-a-brac: Precious Angels figurines, small porcelain pigs, some crushed, others intact, Hot Wheels cars, commemorative plates. I handed my father a birdcage. He looked at it, and opened its front gate. He removed a tiny pig and put the pig in his shirt pocket.

I think in pictures, but I remember you in words, in sentences, fragments, letters, notes, emails, in books with pages bent, overdue to some campus library. You'd prefer that, I think. But I can see you. If I focus, if I squeeze my brain. It's always the same image, you in a white dress shirt, rain-drenched, your black glasses moist and fogged, sitting across from me in first class, nervous for those three hours as our train wobbled through the storm outside, taking us from your Boston to my New York. Our Northeast Corridor. Did you know I lied? I didn't have tickets. I didn't pay. You were in the toilet, and I scammed the conductor, batted my eyes, asked for help with this misunderstanding, and he melted faster than you ever did. Theft of service, technically, but you never suspected. You were an innocent, the sin was all mine. We didn't talk. We dried. I piled my magazines into a ziggurat on the floor between us. My *Cosmos*. My *Vogues*. I chewed through them, tearing out the prettiest models, the sauciest tips. You read one book. Reinhold Niebuhr. *Moral Man and Immoral Society.*

Cleaning was cage, cage, another cage, until we were four feet in. We both stank. My laces were undone. When you're skinny, tying your shoes is nothing, forgettable, like licking a stamp or chopping an onion. But you can never lose yourself when you're fat. You feel everything. You feel your neck. You feel your thighs. You feel your stomach flop over, you feel every drop on your skin, and you don't know if it's sweat or if you're dirty. You tie your shoes as fast as you can.

The floor was becoming visible: a red Oriental rug, trimmed with Arabic calligraphy, curly letters looping over and into themselves like snakes. Mason jars and paper cups. Sun-lit crates of pampers. I chucked boxes of dishwashing powder, sea sponges dyed brown. An ancient yellow dress, washing tag in Spanish. My dad offered me fifty bucks for us to quit, to go home. I kissed his forehead and told him, "No."

Only six feet in. 10:00am. This song needed a faster beat. I ripped ten garbage bags off our roll and laid them, mouth open, in a line from the door to the shore of trash. I threw what was in front of me—a Coleman lantern, a blue book called *Cocina al minuto*—into the first bag. My father looked tired in the sun. He clinched the bag with a bread wrapper, and held the next one open. Now: A ceramic bowl, fire engine red. It looked catalog-fresh. I imagined that red bowl filling with blue pills. I dropped the bowl into the bag, and it shattered. Then a pressure cooker, a Mr. Coffee, and my father held the next bag. My hands plunged into trash, and it was all awareness. My stomach creasing into thirds, my thighs knocking together, sweat draining down my neck, and there: my shadow, spilling ahead, betraying me, more wide than long, a big gray blob cast over all this crap.

More rug. Splatters of motor oil. My father got beer from the truck. Mini-Budweisers, eight ounces, each the size of a fist.

"How do you drink it?" I asked. I'd been stealing his beer for years. But I wasn't teasing. It's a gift to let others think you're simple, to allow them a slice of rescue.

"Slam it. You sip a cold beer, slam a hot one."

He opened my beer can, then his.

"I'm counting to three," he said. "First one wins!"

"Ready!" I told him, locking my eyes onto his, until he looked away.

"Three—two—"

I chugged, booze in the gullet. He was going to let me win, but I needed to cheat. You taught me that we only have the agency we seize.

Saltines. A molded humidifier. A box of ancient certificates, the word *Habana,* the word *matrimonio.* Another half hour and we'd cleared out twelve feet. The garbage rose ahead of us: we stood at the base of the crest. Where did you find your words? You never fell sick: you went awry. A tryst for me was a rendezvous for you. What would you have told the girl crossing this sea of garbage? Godspeed? Excelsior? I pulled out a pile of pants. Wool trousers. Some bearing tags, some lined with underwear. Handkerchiefs. Linen pants. I plunged my hand into a suit and hit wood. First time I yelled fuck in front of my dad. He saw me kissing my hand. I cleared off the suit. There was a curved wooden surface, painted beige, Apple *IIe* beige. I removed tangles of sweaters, and saw that the wood curved upwards until its peak.

It was the bottom of a boat.

My father sucked his cheeks into a fish face. He rapped on the exposed hull, which gave the hollow report of a watermelon. He looked back at me, his expression miming what-the-fuck, my own saying who-the-hell-knows.

He peeled a pair of Raimundo's long johns off the boat and tossed it down the hall. I laid my hand on wood. It was hot, very hot, that deep summer burn of a bus stop seat in a black neighborhood. I took my father's right glove—we were both lefties—and we went to it, clearing the boat. He had the fore, I the aft. I was bent over, my shirt crawling upwards, my Dolphins sweats slothing down. My dad's clothes fit just right. We flung off duffel bags, advertising circulars, guayaberas, and as the boat shed its skin, we could see it—denuded, a mildewed vessel, capsized before us, the memory of the sea cracked into its paint. The boat was twelve feet long, five feet deep, and just as wide—wider than any door or window. A naked woman was painted on the front. She lay on her stomach, facing forward, afraid of nothing, the black paint of her hair gliding over the blotted pink of her body. Laurels on her head, and she was blowing into a conch shell, a string of notes tumbling out, a treble clef fogged at the end. Behind her, silver paint, brushed cursive reading "DIOS Y PACIENCIA."

I looked at my father. He squinted in the glare of the sun, and sweat that masqueraded as tears gathered in the wrinkles around his eyes.

"Dad, we got to get rid of this."

"But it's his boat."

"Whose boat?"

"From Cuba."

DIOS Y PACIENCIA—my father traced the words on the hull, the forefinger of his yellow glove crawling over the cursive D. Sweat crossed my stomach and met in the heavy of my back. I saw my dad's collarbones, obvious and attentive; how many houses would I have to clean for my collarbones to show? You could tell a man painted the naked woman. Pinched waist, heavy breasts, seashell top. My bra was from K-mart, almost-B.

I spotted a metal pole. The pole was scalding. But I held on. What's deadly about an open wire is that it constricts your muscles, your hand clamps shut around the current, and you clutch onto the shock until someone saves you. My father's finger was starting on Y, and I smashed the pole right on the woman. He snapped: "Claudia!" But the paint didn't even chip.

I let the silence hang, and my father went back to tracing the letters, then he stopped. His eyes fixed on the curve where the sides of the boat converged.

"We've got to save it," he said.

The air was seared and thick. I loosened the drawstring on my sweatpants.

"You can't be serious."

"You know when Mom died? I threw away her clothes. Her books. Her necklaces. There was nothing, but everything was so clean, remember?"

I didn't. I was four. She wasn't even a memory.

"Of course I remember."

My dad muttered—"Where is a crowbar? I need a crowbar"—and zigzagged through the room of trash, turning up piles, plunging hands into garbage. He yelled at a rake. Cursed at a broom. And then he found a chisel. He took my hand—yellow glove in yellow glove—and walked me around the boat. "Remember everything," he said, rapping the boat with the chisel. "Because we're going to put her back together."

"We need to get rid of it."

"This is how we'll keep her."

I wanted to strike the boat again. To crack a hole. To murder that painted bitch. But then my legs crossed themselves. An order from my bladder, a pinch above my groin. Is it the same for men? Because you feel like you drank a pool. Like you're about to pop. It burns. And there's this pressure, this pain in you, this little gremlin grabbing your insides and squeezing.

I ran to the hallway. It was clogged like an artery, crammed with air conditioners and joint-compound buckets, and I slithered through the narrow opening, my back to the wall, shuffling side-ways, hunting for the toilet.

Door one. Nothing. Garbage and a water heater.

Door two. A bedroom. Black-mold mattress and garbage.

Door three. The bathroom was white, white walls, white sink, with a white rubber mat in front of the white tub. It was small, with a little window, and a mirror opposite the toilet, but it was empty, no cans of combs, no bundles of newspaper.

I pulled down my sweats. It was one of those foam seats and I sank into it, and my thighs squeezed against each other so I couldn't see the water. I felt that little tremor right before you pee, where the pressure is unbearable, and relief is an instant away, but now I also felt a gurgle in my stomach, the rumblings of number two. Maybe it was gas. Maybe it was a false alarm. Maybe I could hold it till home.

Because at home I had a routine. It helped. Crack the window, run the water. Drop my pants and sit. And I'd cough, cough in spurts, so they'd think the fat girl was clearing her throat, not scrounging for stray flecks of shame. And I'd count too. I wanted out by sixty. But if my stomach, my bowels, my plumbing, went awry, if they boiled infernal, I would count to two hundred. Five hundred. And I would get confused—540, 541—and think I was counting my weight. Finish. Clean. Pants up. Wash my hands, gargle, and spill Listerine to cover the smell.

You once brought a *Harper's* to the bathroom. You took twenty minutes: a cover article, a pair of reviews. How could you read there? You must feel alone, an empty mind, a perfect calm, a chance to read up on blood diamonds, or the perils of floating exchange rates. I never felt alone. I always felt watched, like an animal narrated on *Nature:* "This is Claudia, an unusually sized primate, in chronic disequilibrium." There'd be me, half-naked, stuck in the seat like a cork, expelling myself, not being able to see below, my thighs in the way, sitting in a stench that was my gauge how it was going down there, a kind of braille. All this because there is so much of you, your mass and being measured in tissue paper unfurled, an endless scroll.

You men are so simple. You want to read, to fuck, and to be broken.

I ran the water. Just in case. My hands were under my thighs, fingers curling under the toilet seat. I held my breath and started to pee. Instantly: a feeling of peace. An envelope of grace. That pinch between my legs, slackening like a dying cramp. This bliss stretched maybe fifteen seconds, but it could have been hours. My legs felt so cold, and I exhaled, my breath heavy with relief. Safe. I bent down to pull up my sweats, then—a whir in my guts. There was no push, no effort, I couldn't even feel it leave, just a trap door open and everything inside of me spilling down into the bowl. My shirt had risen up between my breasts and my navel, and my middle was flopped out, basted with sweat.

It was in pieces and sludge and stank like death in a house that already smelled like the end. Was I done? A question mark hovered in front of me: a big dot, with a curve above, a scythe ready to cut off my pride. The window had a yellow frame. No breeze. I looked for a bird, but there was just the flat blue of the sky, free of unemployed clouds, a single color floating in the permanent heat.

I rocked from side-to-side, my thighs wet from the sweat of work and the damp of backsplash. A little more crept out, a liquid coda, the last of what I held.

I used a roll of toilet paper. When you're thin, you need a few sheets, single ply. But when you're fat, you don't know. You start at the middle, and you use sheet upon sheet. Then you pull yourself wide with one hand, and the other, paper-gloved, hunting for something foul, and wiping clean the center and then the cornea, and the whole orbit of your rear, all damp with the sweat that sticks to you forever like radiation. And with all that gone, another run, another wipe, scanning for leftovers, scanning randomly, without a plan, stochastically you would say, just in case, like a metal detector on the beach. You know, sometimes after I'd finish, after I'd wipe, I'd worry I still wasn't clean, and I would take a shower. And sometimes, the water coursed down my leg like rust.

The bathroom tiles gleamed. Even the grout between the tiles, those little lines that always get dirty, they gleamed too. At least, I remember they did.

I bent over, one hand on the floor, the other cleaning, spelunking, looking for shit inside of me, or shit-water tucked into a skin flap. I made a mistake. I looked up. My reflection occupied the width of the mirror, but maybe it wasn't me ahead, maybe this was a window instead of a mirror, maybe this sad mass, all flesh, no dignity, maybe it was someone else. But she stared back at me, her face starting with recognition and ending in horror.

Your own face asked before your mouth did. I packed my suitcase in silence, folding my life away from you by halves. Then: "Why?" The only angry word you ever said. I locked my eyes on a stack of books, the spines' blue leather, a pile of treatises pockmarked with your handwriting. My hands rolled up a pair of skinny jeans, wedging them behind a litter of socks. I looked so pretty that day, do you remember? "It's just that we need time apart," I said. You knew I was bullshitting. I turned my back and kept folding until you left the room. Why? Because you were so good to me. My prize and my challenge. And when you turned in your collar, my thrill became triumph: I'd defeated God as I'd defeated the body He gave me. And now that I'd won, it was over.

Toilet paper floated in the bowl, and I pulled up my panties. The filth that had been within me drifted in the water.

I flushed.

The glug of the cistern. The whirlpool spiraled, the pipes gushed. But the water didn't descend. It hesitated at a level, and then it rose. I felt the breath of Satan as all of it, this wet stew, climbed up the bowl. I flushed again but it wouldn't stop. I couldn't find a plunger in the bathroom, but I bet there was a box of twenty outside. I took the lid off the tank and jiggled the black plastic float. I coughed a prayer, but the water swelled higher.

The knob behind the toilet. It was rusted, a dead orange. I tried turning it. Stuck. I tried harder. The grooves of the knob pressed into my palm, but it wouldn't budge. I grabbed it with both hands. I groaned, pushed, put my weight behind it—and the knob loosened, squeaking clockwise.

But it didn't matter. The water kept rising, creeping up to the lip of bowl, the mess bobbing above the surface like apples.

My reflection looked at me, disappointed.

We were going to get rid of that fucking boat.

Nice Parts

Alyssa Lempesis
GLUE, PLASTIC, FABRIC, ACRYLIC MEDIUM, RUBBER, DYE

Whether or Not the Weather Is a Bellwether of a Blizzard in my Brain

Bryan Valenzuela

INK, ACRYLIC, WATERCOLOR, GEL TRANSFER ON ARCHES WATERCOLOR PAPER

40" X 26"

Chew

Kayleb Rae Candrilli

When my mother chewed off
her own hands it was because
she convinced herself each finger
was the penis of a man
who would have treated her
better. She would tick
them off as she sucked
and chewed:

> *X, and X, and X,*
> *and he's a lawyer now,*
> *and he's a business owner,*
> *and the other's just plain kind.*

She would hum while she fellated
each little bit of herself. And every
mistake she'd ever made would swell
in her mouth before its castration.

When my father ripped the wedding ring
off my mother's last remaining finger
he threw it into the forest.

For years, I thought I saw it glinting there,
until my mother opened her mouth to cry

out for help, until I saw that that ring
had landed inside her, until I saw it

> vice-clamp-cock-ringed
> around her esophagus.

Until I heard nothing at all from her,
because it's hard to talk without your hands.

Dowsing

Kristian O'Hare

In the distance, he appears, almost an apparition, a white cherub in a black tee shirt; he wears no pants, butt naked. As he approaches, I see a cock ring holding up a stub of an erection, a stout vigorous stem points like a divining rod. His balls bulbous with an unnatural swollenness, two wrinkled baby cabbages crested with long white hairs. I stand impatiently at 18th street and Church, for the J Church Muni, staring at my phone, waiting for a text, but nothing. The fog settles, a filmy white mist over the flannel red of the flowering gum trees. He pokes toward Dolores Park in a puttered trance. Perhaps he is on drugs or maybe just ripe with desire. He disappears into the palm trees, only the silver glow of his white sneakers left when my phone lights up *Working late tonight.*

Later, at home, in bed, I remove my underpants, a slight rubbing turns into a dry jerk off to some bareback porn I found on one of those free amateur sites: I try not to focus on the room messy with empty Monster energy drink cans and bottles of amyl nitrate, or the natty stuffed animal collection. There is a hirsute man, on his hands and knees, who eagerly awaits while the camera focuses on the pileous anther, a dilated petal-like stamen, a fissure like a pink lady's slipper. I close my eyes and imagine a city full of ghosts. They aren't translucent and floating like the ghosts in the movies. They are a heavy paper, bruised inky purple, and vermillion veined. They aren't light and airy; they are clumsy, bumping into benches and brushing against the mottled bark of the Brisbane box trees. Some lie in the park on top of each other, not like lovers but like trash, stuck together, gathering, in flaccid heaps. I try to sleep, without my underpants, a phone in my hand, quiet, unlit. That man is still out there, still dowsing the streets.

Feast Days

Suzanne Rivecca
2016 Gina Berriault Award Winner

<u>Agenda Item 4, File #160764</u>

Transcript of a direct address to The San Francisco Board of Supervisors'
Public Safety and Neighborhood Services Committee, by Kevin "White Ti-
ger" Larabee, Founder & CEO of Meeblyboo, Inc, during a public hearing
on "Hunger Abatement via NOUXtrition: a proposed city ordinance to de-
cree NOUXtrition, a meal replacement in the form of a soluble pellet, the
'designated sustenance' for San Francisco's indigent population."

Supervisors, I'm honored to be here today representing my company, Meeblyboo, which began in my buddy Glenn's parents' bonus room in a subdivision of Bloomington, Indiana in 2010. I won't bore you with the details of Meeblyboo's genesis—although it's an amazing story, with a lot of hijinks, and would probably make a much more original and authentically *human* movie than any of the five million they've made about Jobs—because I'm not here to talk about my humble beginnings. I'm here to talk about a different, but no less significant, beginning. I'm here to talk about NOUXtrition. What is NOUXtrition? Well, as far as you're concerned, the definition is twofold: in a short-term sense, it's the pinnacle of your careers in public service; in the long-term, it's a revolution. The *good* kind. Not the rioting kind.

First of all, though, I cannot ignore the fact that this hearing has generated major public interest. Therefore, on behalf of myself and my colleagues, who since our arrival in this community have labored under a cloud of distrust and misinformation, I'd be remiss if I didn't take this opportunity to dispel, once and for all, on the record and in the presence of a diverse and uniquely *vocal* sampling of San Francisco residents as well as several media outlets of varying levels of populist bias *and* our esteemed legislative body, a few myths that plague my industry: that we all come from privilege; that we live in luxury and lack diversity; that we exist in an insulated bubble of self-perpetuating homogeneity; that we loll around on beanbags all day throwing circus peanuts into each other's open mouths; that we are bereft of social graces and obsessed with short-term solutions; that our companies' names are mere random mashups of magnetic-poetry fragments clumsily juxtaposed on some dorm-room mini-fridge of a crisp New Haven eve; that we invent 'problems' of staggeringly trifling triviality, rickety and flammable as strawmen, and then traffic in their specious solutions, which we also spin out of straw; that we cynically appropriate certain concepts—concepts rife with associations of inclusion and a refreshing lack of ceremony, concepts such as "sharing"—and use them to convince the human race that every supposed inherent birthright, from water to air to a view of the sky, is actually a biddable commodity, one whose perceived scarcity we carefully engineer before blasphemously re-christening it with a stupid name, trussing it up with fine print and overages, and enshrining it as a golden calf of status-based anxiety for an increasingly globalized, stratified, and hysterically insecure consumer base. This is what I hear, at least.

These are the murmurs that trail me each day as I commute the five blocks from my co-operative residence to Meeblyboo headquarters, riding with my colleagues in what I can only describe, in these times of environmental crisis, as the ultimate carpool. A giant white shuttle bus shepherding, between home and work, a cadre of idealistic young dreamers who hold in their brains the potential to *solve* the environmental crisis. And all the crises that hit this town hardest. The homelessness crisis, and the housing crisis, and the affordability crisis, and the crisis of having no parking, the crisis of having to circle the same fucking hill *twenty times* while you run out of gas, and the crisis of this town being *covered* in dog shit because apparently everyone's too *laid-back* and *flower-power* to pick up after a dog lest they hurt its canine feelings by deeming its excrement not *special* enough to adorn our storied streets or something, and also the crises of disconnection and loneliness and heartbreak and sickness and mortality. We've got a plan to fix it all, folks. Solutions, which I'll discuss today, are in the works, so when you see one of those white shuttles roll down your street, please stop throwing things at it, because there's precious cargo in there. That shuttle bears the men who will save you. And some girls who help a lot, too.

Let me just say one thing about myself. Privileged? I don't know the meaning of the word. I went to a state school. Not even Big Ten. Our mascot wasn't an animal you can find in nature, because those were all taken by better schools. Our mascot was a fucking owl with antelope horns. An Anteowl. Our most illustrious alumnus was a guy who invented a special gadget intended for extreme outdoorsman; it was a portable toilet, collapsible tent, stovetop, and Segway all in one. Yes, the Swiss Army Knife on Wheels. Except the Swiss Army Knife people sued and he had to change the name to WheeliePoop, which didn't even do justice to the full range of functions the apparatus can perform; plus he got screwed when he sold the patent, so he didn't have enough money to endow entire buildings. He endowed particular articles of furniture, which were affixed with plaques bearing the name of his product. You want to talk about privilege, Supervisors and constituents? I didn't feel too privileged when I was sitting on the WheeliePoop Endowed Papa-san Chair in the student union, wearing a lacrosse uniform with an Anteowl on it and dreaming of a brighter future.

As for diversity, I have a passion for it, one that took unlikely root and flourished in a soil of privation, at the aforementioned state school whose dining hall didn't even have a soft-serve ice cream machine. As a sophomore, I founded an entirely new social club, a tech fraternity, and christened it HymenHack. For the benefit of the unschooled: the founding members of HymenHack created an algorithm that ranks all incoming freshman girls according to the likelihood that they are virgins; if they are deemed to be so, it goes a step further by hypothesizing the expiration date of that impediment, *and* each deflowering's probable venue, based on certain telling variables. It has an eighty-eight percent accuracy rate, and yes, that *is* adjusted to accommodate manipulation and unreliable reportage. The demographic information and raw data alone are a gold mine for advertising agencies and the behavioral sciences alike. Today, 544 affiliate chapters of HymenHack exist in universities across the country, and you'll find faces of every color, from white to off-white to a kind of light Frappuccino hue, in all of them, and that's because I set a standard. I worked tirelessly to diversify the inaugural chapter, going so far as to recruit three Southeast Asians, one half-Samoan, and one ambiguously ethnic Communications major who described his skin tone and heritage as "pan-swarthy."

Imagine! Young men of all—or least of several—races, coming together to synthesize surreptitiously-obtained data with the common goal of demystifying the unifying signifiers of the most individually particular, life-altering, and joyous rite of passage in the journey of a coed. It's not just an algorithm, Supervisors. It's a celebration of life and a bridge to understanding. In other words, it's *information.* And information is currency. Information is also a dove of peace. Additionally, it's power. Another thing it is: a passport to different worlds. One that negates the differences of those worlds and elevates them to a plane of blissful interchangeability. In addition, it's also the Rosetta Stone, *and* the mother tongue of all of humanity. And the only home and parent and lover we'll ever need. And that is why we traffic in it.

Now, I can roll with the punches. I didn't get where I am today by having a thin skin. But there's one myth that really gets me, that actually *hurts.* And it's this: that we're naïve to think we can change the world. *That we're naïve.*

I hate to break it to you, but we already *have* changed the world. And we're not stopping anytime soon.

Let me back up a bit and explain a little something about Meeblyboo. When Glenn and I founded this start-up, we chose the name because we didn't know what it was going to do—what, I suppose you could say, we'd actually be *starting up*—and so Meeblyboo seemed to embody the playfully joyful aimlessness of our enterprise, while also leaving the door open for any number of exciting possibilities. Finally, we decided that Meeblyboo would focus on the *virtual* experience.

Now, Glenn is a purist, a true ascetic; he lives what he creates. He's going to die on top of a mountain, on his terms. He's the man I admire most in the world. And he's obsessed with how perception can shape reality. Most people are wedded to the opposite concept: that reality creates certain perceptions. Look where that's gotten us. If you want proof, just walk from City Hall to United Nations Plaza. Just once. You're going to see a lot of people smoking crack and shitting themselves. And you're going to cross the street to avoid them. And they're going to keep smoking crack and shitting themselves. But what if, when you looked at them, you saw *something else*? Something *non-threatening*, something you could understand? And vice versa?

Thanks to Glenn, we know *what if.* In the dark days of 2012, he invented Meeblyboo's famous Leveling Lenses. The early prototype was strapped to the forehead like a pith helmet, with two telescopic viewfinders protruding from each eye socket; and the pioneers who wore this trial version out in public were targeted by the masses with a coordinated onslaught of vigilante disenfranchisement. So the Meeblyboo crew labored to make our invention stealthier. One morning, after waffle service at the office Roundtable, Glenn plunked down in front of us a tiny, transparent disc, the size and color of a fingernail. The object was as small and anticlimactically insubstantial as Willy Wonka's tiny Gobstopper: a wan spitball ejected by the massive, bombastically clanging machinery of our collective vision.

"This is it," Glenn said. "This is the final version."

"It looks like a like contact lens," I said.

And he replied, in a tone of drained, weightless triumph that would have been grating under less extraordinary circumstances, "It is."

Let me explain the genius of the Leveling Lenses in layman's terms. Each pair is activated by and connected to one's mobile device, via the downloading of the Leveling App. The app can discern your exact location at any given time by pinpointing your street coordinates, and in addition, it is equipped with an exquisite sensitivity to one's topographical environment and the human figures that populate it. In short, it can tell if any given human figure in your vicinity is a prime candidate for obfuscation—or, more accurately, for visual neutralization and improvement. For example, if a human figure is prone on the ground, he or she is likely to be such a candidate; similarly, if the figure is situated in a doorway, or merely lurks and loiters instead of walking briskly and purposefully, or if its movements are erratic and sloppy, or if it's emitting sounds at high decibels with no detectable respondent, chances are high the lenses' effect will be activated. Thanks to the exhaustive and intricately detailed amount of kinesthetic, sonic, and sensory data we've collected on the commonalities, in bearing and affect, of the indigent population, the lenses have a ninety-nine percent accuracy rate in identifying candidates appropriate for virtual defusing.

If I put in my Leveling Lenses and strolled down to UN Plaza right now, Supervisors, I wouldn't see a bunch of hobos. I would not be distracted by the planes of a face, by eyes, by the unreadable vagaries of expression. I'd see a delightful image, duplicated as many times as necessary, superimposed across every redundant visage with a gloriously viral universalism transcending race and creed. I'd see a series of digitally-generated replacement faces. These are round genderless orbs of indeterminate ethnicity, hairless taupe spheres radiating level-eyed neutrality, with a noncommittal line for a mouth. And beside each sphere, hovering jauntily as if hoisted high by the vagrant's unseen hand: a cunning little bindle stick.

Thanks to our Community Benefit contract with the city, it goes both ways. It was Glenn who conceived of the pop-up clinic. We shepherded every vagrant he could find, dogs and duffels and all, through the clinic's doors. We gave them hot coffee, donuts, exercise balls to sit on, and a throwback TV that played reruns of *Sanford and Son*. Most just fell asleep. And when it was their turn to be evaluated, they followed our "optician" into the examining room, and allowed their eyes to be fitted with a free pair of Leveling Lenses and a mobile app-enabled device. These special limited-edition lenses, in contrast to the prototype model, had been customized to identify *us*, the Meeblyboo crew. In addition to a general sameness of bearing—a slight slouch, exacerbated by a messenger bag—and haircut and sartorial choices, we apparently share, as extensive facial scanning and analysis revealed, a default expression. Glenn even commissioned a bronze cast of it, for his office. It's rather noble-looking, if I do say so myself, and conveys the avidly bug-eyed, pained preoccupation of a Galileo, or a Gates.

But thanks to the lenses, the trial participants didn't see this expression when they looked at us. They didn't see the clear signs that we'd come so much farther than they had, and accomplished so much. All they saw was a constellation of little circle-faces, each untainted by distinguishing disfigurements. Just a beige orb, frankly friendly as a thumbprint. And, the sole modification: off to one side, a tiny hovering keyboard. And these people came to understand that, in our world, their offensive physicality is virtual, and therefore no longer offensive. They understood that the main impediments to their assimilation—their putrid bodies ceaselessly demanding to be furnished with the means to eat and drink and shit—were in the process of being negated.

Next to go, after the faces, was the food. Thus, NOUXtrition was born.

Before I go any further, I want to make one thing clear: no one should be "gotten rid of." Right? That's a no-brainer. I grew up watching the History Channel, and if there's one thing I learned, it's that if you ascend to prominence you'd better stay on the right side of history. Or else they'll make you look like a total asshole fifty years hence on TV. So, let me state this for the record: every person's life has equal value. But in my opinion, humanism without realism is actually inhumane. Why? Because it willfully ignores certain ungovernable differences between subsets of people, differences that do not—I repeat, *do not*—imply that any one group is less worthy, but *do* indicate that not all of us are constitutionally *equipped* to bear an equal burden of responsible citizenship, or to graciously adjust our tiny, colorful individual derangements so as to assimilate, as it were, into the larger holistic consciousness of an actual community of people. Particularly a community of people forced to co-exist in a radius of seven square miles crisscrossed by fault lines, built on landfill, helmed by shark-infested waters, and restricted by building codes so precious they may well have been designed for the ceramic Victorian Christmas village my grandma has on her coffee table. It boils down to this: Everyone deserves to live, but not necessarily to live *here,* in a way that grosses out the rest of us. And just as people outgrow their cities, there are circumstances in which cities outgrow their people.

Now, it's no secret that this town has a lot of hungry people. Unfortunately, when those people get fed, they tend to defecate. And a significant portion of this subpopulation is at elevated risk of defecating publicly. And then there's the enormous, convoluted, and exorbitant city-subsidized machinery perpetuating an endless cycle of feed/shit/cleanup, with no end in sight.

The direness of this daily reality convinced me and Glenn that the Leveling Lenses, however revolutionary in themselves, primarily served to illuminate a larger principle, one that demanded a larger solution. The need to pare down. The need to simplify. These are not austerity measures. These are reductions, potent as a once-watery broth simmered to a syrupy, curative essence.

Again, let me reiterate: we're not making anyone disappear. We're just making the worst things *about* them disappear, and replacing a million dehumanizing options with one *empowering* option.

This brings me to the nuts and bolts of NOUXtrition. As I said, it's Glenn's baby. And Glenn dreamed big. His ultimate fantasy was for NOUXtrition to be adopted as the sole means of subsistence for everyone, globally. He said famine will be abolished, pasturelands and orchards will be utilized for the cultivation of semiconductor-grade silicon, and perhaps most importantly, all sentimental baggage will be drained from the concept of nourishment.

"Do you know what this means?" he said to me. "Food won't be used as a weapon anymore, or as a comfort. Because aren't the two things interchangeable?"

Believe me, I applaud Glenn's egalitarian spirit. But we need to pace ourselves. While we strongly encourage the general populace to at least incorporate NOUXtrition into your diets—it's an amazing weight-loss tool, for one thing—we firmly believe that, by dint of choosing to shit indoors, most of us have earned the right to culinary autonomy.

As for the rest, until they decide to clean up their act, it's only fair that their consumption be restricted to NOUXtrition: a pellet that dissolves in the mouth and expands in the stomach to create a sensation of fullness for at least eight hours, while providing the minimum of recommended RDA for maintenance of human life and functioning. Here's the best part: if one subsists solely on the NOUXtrition pellet, one's waste products will exit the body discreetly and inoffensively, encased in a charcoal-infused, odorless biodegradable sac—painless to excrete, I assure you—that resembles nothing so much as a small latex balloon, and can be knotted up and discarded after elimination. These sacs can then be tossed into any number of "MicroPooplets": little patches of fortified soil, staggered at two-block intervals in our city's most plagued districts, for the convenience of the outdoor eliminators. Once an elimination sac is tossed on the soil, it will commence breaking down, eventually deliquescing into a super-charged "fertilizer bomb" that will yield a harvest of glorious California poppies (or succulents, or clematis, or monkey flowers: the future incarnation of his ordure will be entirely the choice of each eliminator, just one of many ways our system fosters the individual empowerment of those in need). Thus, the main polluters of our landscape will become its most reliable beautifiers.

To discourage the illicit consumption of normal food, each pellet includes a chemical that induces six hours of sanitary-and-silent suffering (SSS)—and I mean that literally, because side effects include temporary mutism, but *don't* include the expulsion of bodily fluids, because that would kind of defeat the purpose, right?—within ten minutes of ingesting any non-pellet substance. (Let me assure you that the canine version of NOUXtrition, intended for the pets of the indigent, does not contain this chemical. We're not monsters; and besides, animals are innocent of their masters' lifestyle choices. As our detractors are fond of reminding us at every turn, this *is* the City of St. Francis.)

This leads us to the hard questions. *How* would we go about mandating the ingestion of a daily pellet among a notoriously ornery and transient population? Well, the first step is to create *demand*. Look at methadone clinics. Why do people stand in line for hours to drink a liquefied opiate from a dixie cup? Because they're in withdrawal. Within twelve hours of abstaining from NOUXtrition, an unpleasant skin-crawling sensation sets in that can only be alleviated by another dose of NOUXtrition. Conveniently, if someone finds himself in dire need of NOUXtrition, he can get his "fix" immediately, via a special Meeblyboo app that alerts him to the nearest pellet-dispensing kiosk in the vicinity. And if a consumer earns the right to transition out of the NOUXtrition program—via gainful employment, perhaps, or acquisition of market-rate housing, or permanent exile from the city and its environs——that person will, on a case-by-case basis, be eligible to receive an injection that neutralizes the withdrawal response. So that's step one. Step two: remove other options. In short, there will be nothing else on the menu.

There's one final thing. It's a more recent modification to the program, facilitated by a painful, albeit cathartic, reckoning. I wish Glenn could be here to tell you about it himself. But he can't. Because here's the thing about Glenn. Pardon my bluntness, but Glenn lost his goddamn mind. Glenn is kind of *not in the picture* at the moment. Let me tell you about the last time I saw Glenn, about six months ago. Now, keep in mind, this was after weeks and weeks of escalating weirdness on his part. He insisted on subsisting on NOUXtrition spiked with a daily dose of ayahuasca: a cocktail he'd created solely for his own consumption because he thought it'd exorcise all subjective and emotional associations from his perception and let him see the world not as he'd been conditioned to see it, and not as it actually was, but as it *could* be if allowed to evolve uninfluenced by memories or attachments or appetites, and he just wanted to *glimpse* this vision for reference, to screenshot it, if you will, like some kind of dispatch from a utopian crystal ball that he could use as a blueprint for the future, but he kind of got stuck in some limbo between that world and this one. And he was basically turning into a hologram, appearing to us like Obi-wan without warning, on the street or in the halls, so frail and holy his edges seemed pixilated, saying things like, "Someday we'll all be made of feldspar," and "If you're going to eat that sandwich, you might as well just fellate a Colombian warlord." Usually, the food item he'd be referencing was actually a stapler, or an iPad. And then I ran into him one night in the kitchen of our co-living space, Minimalista, where he'd invented NOUXtrition in the first place, and I'll never forget the figure he cut: he was gaunt and haunted, with the long fanatical face of an ungulate in mating season, and he asked me to take him upstairs to his micro-unit and "tuck him into bed," which I did, smoothing his bangs across his forehead and scooting his sleeping-drawer into the wall, feet-first, so that only his pious, elongated, hairy head protruded from the slot, and he said to me, "All I ever wanted to do was make the world better."

"You *have*, Glenn," I told him, but he wouldn't listen. He just kept trying to tell me some story about being a kid in Little League and how his dad was his coach and the grass was a different green back then—in his words, "so verdant it was almost *noxious* in its lurid saturation, the green of arsenic, the green of absinthe, so green I could taste this vegetal acidity on the back of my tongue when I looked at it, Kevin!"—and then he just went off. He was just this crazy, babbling, disembodied head sticking out of a wall, recounting what various things tasted like on some night in 1996 when he and the other Baskin Robbins Bombers, or whatever they were called, won the big game at the sandlot in Peoria. He kept talking about the concession stand, how you could get ten red licorice shoelaces for a penny each and hold them in your fist like a wilting bouquet, and this other thing that was, like, a bunch of edible chalky sticks that you'd dip in a packet of grape powder, and how Nerds came in these little boxes with separate slots for each flavor and they were all gnarled and nuggety and shellacked-looking, and how they felt so amazing in the mouth. And then he was crying, and it was really messed up, and he kept saying to me, or at least I think this is what he said but he was crying so hard I could barely understand him, but I think he said, "There's some part of me that's still here and I don't want to be here."

And I don't know if he meant he didn't want to be of this world anymore, or he didn't want to experience the tyranny of tactility and sensation anymore. I don't know. But the important thing is this: he said it was just *some part of him* that posed a problem. And I know how that feels, to have part of you held hostage by some possessive force of gravity, tethered to the ground while the rest of you floats above, like a balloon, and waits for that part to get lighter. And it just doesn't. And there's no separating from it. So the heavy part, even if it's the smallest part of you, can keep you from ascending. And the reason it's so heavy is because it contains all the stuff about you that's insoluble. Irrelevant and counterproductive, but insoluble. All that shit: like how no one would sit with you at lunch and how the shame you felt was less on your own behalf and more on your mom's, how confused and hurt and aggrieved she'd be at having raised a kid other kids make fun of, how she'd see it as a failure of her own, and the silvery smog of beer on your dad's breath when he'd fall asleep on the couch with his glasses on and infomercials blaring, with a copy of *Glamour* on his chest because he had three daughters and had gotten into the habit of uncomplainingly and anthropologically reading whatever girly dreck they left lying around, instead of going out and buying some magazine *he* was actually interested in, and how

you realized at some point, maybe when you were thirteen or so and
your dad got laid off, that you belong to a tribe of people who drink
the whey while everyone else gets the cream, a family of self-effacers, of
nice people too civil to fight and too smart to kowtow, fated to circle the
drain in resentment and hurt and paralysis and the worst part was they
knew they deserved better but no one would give them a fucking chance
and they also knew exactly *why*: because they were nondescript, because
they were decent and smart but had flaws, like female pattern baldness
or a weak chin or a penchant for deflection, flaws that kept them from
being *dynamic*, flashy, "sexy," the kind of people who get listened to or
get promoted or get good service in restaurants. And it's insane, how the
full despairing import of this fuckery can be embodied and transmit-
ted, with dismal immediacy, by the unctuous slick of ice cream on the
tongue: your family's weekly treat, soured by your very consciousness
of the fact it *was* a treat, an exception to the grey endurance of your
daily lot, soured by the earnest pleasure and anticipation with which
its presence was heralded—"We're going to Swirly's tonight!"—and oh
God your dad and mom, losing themselves for a minute of debased and
savoring abandon, tongues slowly, reverently dragging along a mound
of butter pecan in a flyspecked booth while a Jukebox played something
horribly incongruous, like George Michael's "I Want Your Sex," and
how depressed you were by their innocent pleasure while at the same
time wanting fiercely to protect it, as you would any cold, sweet illusion that gives momentary respite to the blameless and damned. That,
Supervisors, is the heavy part. That's the part that keeps us separated,
keeps us isolated, makes us attach arbitrary meaning to things that don't
matter. And the reason gravity clings so tightly to this psychic landfill is
because gravity, like all biological imperatives, is a parasite looking for a
host. It seizes any chance to bring you down.

Anyway, Glenn just kept crying and ranting about candy and how
things smelled until he couldn't function, and now he's in a very nice fa-
cility in Healdsburg, working it out. And what happened to Glenn isn't
unique. He invented something amazing, but his mistake was trying
to make its practical implementation abide by the same cosmic ratio-

nale that facilitated its creation. Every idealist loses his mind eventually. Once this happens, the unsung drudgery of the pragmatist begins. In short, this is where I come in. In case you were wondering, that's why they call me White Tiger. I'm a rarity. You could even call me endangered. I'm the one man in this operation—perhaps the one man in this industry—with the ability to take the extraordinary and make it ordinary. And no, I don't have the order mixed up. Everyone always asks that.

That's not to say I'm not a dreamer. Believe me, I dream of a day in which our teeth soften from lack of use, until eventually our decedents will be born with those bony primitive protuberances, obsolete as mastodon tusks, fully retracted into their gums: a triumphant evolutionary subversion of that most hackneyed of dreams. I have it all the time: the dream of losing teeth. They just drop out of their sockets at once, like pearls, or I gently tug on one and it comes out in my hand, yielding with such obscene and rotted ease, and I wake up gasping. It feels so real. I've had it since I was five years old, and it gets worse and more frequent the more stressed I am, and I am so fucking sick of trying to figure out why my brain does this to me, and why I feel like dying when I see a pigeon pecking a discarded bagel, and why my heart sinks when I see an extremely old couple all dressed up for dinner and wielding their silverware really slowly and carefully at some frenetic and garish chain restaurant, and why I keep ending up in the same place emotionally—a place of shaken, hunted blankness, a sort of agitated aversion to the world's stimuli—and I hate being a conundrum to myself, a bundle of uncontrollable responses, and I look forward to a time when none of us waste energy analyzing the "underlying issues" that manifest in stupid nocturnal hallucinations. *It means you're in a time of transition. It means you're powerless. It means you're scared of change. It means a new beginning.*

I don't want to care what it means! Understand this: in spirit, I'm with Glenn. I no longer want to be moved, against my will, by the poignancy of symbols. I want us to sleep like wolves: in a pack, dreaming only of the objects that could kill or help us.

But it's not time for that. It's too soon. We are crude creatures still, and we must temper our evolution by discriminately coddling, just for now, the parts we can't yet control.

To illustrate, let me tell you a cautionary tale. I mean, in addition to the one I just told about Glenn. Last year, with the endorsement of the mayoral administration, we did a six-month trial for NOUXtrition. We tested it on twenty closely-monitored subjects who subsisted solely on the pellet, with the SSS response activated, for the entire duration of the trial. Five of those subjects were Meeblyboo top brass. One of those five was me. Another of those five was Glenn, but we know how *that* ended. The rest of the subjects were carefully culled from a very special group of mid-Market indigents: people who were hungry, huddled, yearning, the whole deal. We recruited and enrolled these people with the full cooperation of the Mayor's Office of Loving Impoverished Folks, Equally, Liberally, Nicely, & Eternally, SoBeIt, or L.I.F.E.L.I.N.E.S for short. The Office of L.I.F.E.L.I.N.E.S hooked us up with some great folks from their Clean Compassion Crew. For the benefit of those in the gallery, you might know the CCC as the guys and gals who do the real dirty work, guys, consorting with some real odiferous characters all day long and getting them the help they need to, you know, smell better and improve their hygiene. The CCC runs the Soapbox Shower Program, which is that fleet of adorable little outhouses on wheels you see tooling around mid-Market three mornings a week, with the cute little half-moons carved on the front, outside of which the underprivileged line up in droves to wash their cares away with solar-powered hoses that hook right up to the fire hydrants. They just shower right there on the street, where they feel most comfortable! And it's a win-win: they feel good, *we* feel great.

Anyway, the CCC did some awesome outreach for us, screening and hand-selecting fifteen Soapboxers who had the right attitude, motivation, readiness, and mental soundness to be excellent candidates for our trial. In exchange for their participation, each subject got a fully subsidized SRO room for the entire six months, plus regular medical care and forgiveness of any outstanding vagrancy citations. I'm grateful for the D.A.'s cooperation on that last bit, by the way. You can't put a price on a clean slate.

Anyway, one of these participants was a guy I have a real soft spot for. His name's Loam. At least that's what I think he said when he told me his name. Some of these people have "street names," I don't know. If you don't know Loam by name, I guarantee you know him by sight. Or at least you used to. Let me back up. So, Loam would walk around Union Square with a three-tiered menagerie. All day long, he led this zoological triple-decker on a leash: a scrappy, sawdust-colored mutt on the bottom, a calico cat curled up on top of the mutt, and a rat, just chilling on top of the cat. At first I thought they were taxidermy or something, but I got up close for a look, and they were the real deal: the dog licked my hand; the cat yawned; the rat kind of hunched its back up, and its fur was grey with these light brown highlights in the sun, which I wasn't expecting. Anyway, Loam probably raked in at least fifty a day.

When he joined the trial, he asked me if he could drink Thunderbird, and I explained that he'd be restricted to the pellet only, as would Layercake— that was his name for all three of them, like they were one organism; isn't that awesome?—and normally I wouldn't be a stickler about the animals, but we really needed a few non-human models in this thing, just for the sake of data, and what better choice than some prefab freak-show of three discrete species in one?

So everything was okay at first. He'd come to our lab every day, get his vitals checked, and he'd be like, "Hey Kevin, if I die from this pellet bullshit I don't want no shit-flowers at my funeral, you hear? Or at least not my *own.* You better order me some flowers from a real place. If there be a bunch of purple irises at that funeral I'm gonna *know* they're from my shit and I'm gonna haunt you, motherfucker," and I'd be like, "Oh my God, Loam, you are a *national treasure.*"

But around month three or so, he started waning a little. I mean, we all were, to be honest. For one thing, that balloon-sac felt a little. . . invasive in the intestine. I mean, you could actually *feel* it sort of congealing into a cast and forming this tight seal around the contents of your colon, and it was an alien-like, shrink-wrappy, *hardening* feeling, like someone had poured wet plaster in there and it was in a constant state of slowly, crustily drying, and it could make you panic in a pretty primal way. Thankfully, we worked out that kink after the trial. But anyway, I also developed this weird thing where I had to turn the lights off and on fifty times if I was entering or leaving a room. I also apparently started calling my mom at odd hours and telling her "where the documents would be" in case of my death, and she was like, "*What* documents, Kevin?" and I'd just keep yelling about documents, and the next day I'd have no memory of having made these calls. Loam started getting in fights with tourists who tried to feed Layercake their leftover chowder bread bowls or whatever, and what's worse, he'd yell things like "They can't eat that! They're part of a *top-secret trial*," in total violation of the non-disclosure clause. But we overlooked it, because we loved him.

But he got weirder. One time he told me he felt like he had nothing to look forward to.

He said, "Kevin, I'm a hunter. And I got nothing to hunt."

I told him he'd never hunted anything in his life; even when he ate food, he lived on Thunderbird and Del Taco. If anything, I told him, he was a *gatherer*.

"Look," I said, "we're all getting restless. You just have to keep the bigger picture in mind."

He said, and I'll never forget it, "You and me got different pictures."

The reason I'll never forget that is because it's so sad. That's the whole *point* of a bigger picture—it's all-inclusive!

So basically, about four months into the trial Loam stopped checking in at the lab, and he wouldn't answer his door. I had a feeling he was hiding from me, and so I looked in all the places he'd typically *never* go: outside Powell Street BART where those guys pound on buckets all day—the noise scares Layercake, he always said—and Fisherman's Wharf where the creepy dude in the Elmo suit hangs out and acts weirdly sexual, and Coit Tower—it's hard for Layercake to stay intact while climbing stairs—but as it turned out, Loam was where he'd always been: Union Square. It was the last place I went. There he was, on the steps next to the weirdo with the Free Hugs sign, and he was alone.

And the second I saw him, I could tell. He'd eaten. Total SSS: tremors, facial paroxysms, profuse sweating, plus the mutism aspect was in full effect. His mouth worked, but nothing came out.

Early on, before the trial started, I'd deliberately put myself in a state of SSS, because I refused to ask our subjects to endure anything I hadn't endured myself. So I knew what Loam was feeling, and I *particularly* knew he was feeling a curious sensation in his chest, not like a heart attack, but as though a very elegant, tapered, latex-gloved hand was probing the ventricles of his heart and kneading each one, deliberately and intrusively, with this kind of teasing-yet-perversely-fixed insistence on *thoroughness*. I know it sounds very abstract, but trust me, once you feel it, you want to forget your own name and empty your body of blood and replace it with something clear, antiseptic, traceless.

So I knew how he felt, and I knew he couldn't answer me. But I knelt down next to him on the stairs and said, "Loam, it's okay. It'll wear off. In a few hours you'll be good as new. You're still in the trial. Come home."

But he just shook his head. Then I noticed the empty leash in his hand.

"Where's Layercake?" I asked.

He started crying, and it was hard to tell at first because of the facial contortions caused by the SSS, as well as the mutism and the sweating; but when I looked close I saw that his eyes were streaming. He just kept shaking his head. I kept asking the question. He threw his hands up finally, then started trying to draw something in a patch of dirt with a stick, still crying. The picture looked like three blobs stacked on top of each other, with the biggest on the bottom and the smallest on the top. He pointed vehemently at the top blob, the smallest one, then at the middle blob, then held the stick to his mouth and made exaggerated chewing motions as if munching a burrito. Then, with one devastating swipe of the stick, he erased the top blob from the dirt.

It started to dawn on me. "Oh no, Loam," I said.

He kept drawing, scowling in concentration now, his stick stabbing urgently at the dirt. He pointed at the middle blob, then the big bottom one, and made the chewing motion again, and before he even started erasing I knew where this was headed and averted my eyes from the drawing, as if it contained the true horror of the spectacle. Loam put his head in his hands.

The largest blob, the foundation of the three-tiered structure, was still intact.

"Where's the dog?" I asked Loam. He just shook his head. He didn't even have to erase it. I knew from looking at him, so distraught and disagreeably sated, what had happened.

And at first I didn't understand.

"You could have had *anything*," I sputtered. "You could've gone to Trader Joes, for God's sake! You could've dumpster-dived for day-old croissants. It didn't have to be like this!"

But he just kept shaking his head. And I'm not going to claim that Loam reverted to some essential baseness of character, that all his wit and warmth and ingenuity was a thin veneer masking his true brutishness, because that's not the case at all. He was no more brutish, at heart, than I was. And I know this because, as I sat there beside him, having allowed nothing to pass my lips for five months but a daily oatmeal-colored pellet, it became clear to me that I did not pity him. I envied him.

It was very unexpected. But I couldn't deny it. The sight of him sitting there, so recently and shamefully glutted; the blood on his tongue so fresh I could almost smell it; the sheer *matter* of his thick neck, plush and solid with the pulse flinching underneath, a nervously burlesque reflex, *boing boing boing*, like the batting lashes of a cartoon minx. It did something to me. I wanted—as Loam must have wanted, as Layercake must have wanted—the hide, and the bones, and the blood. It was all I could do not to seize him. At that moment, all that saved me was the knowledge that I *understood* him completely, that there was no need for words, and, for perhaps the first time in my life, my terrible dead weight, my heaviest parts, were in utter sympathetic concert with those of another person—and they seemed, by virtue of that liquefying recognition, almost like assets. As if this sensation—sitting next to someone and feeling their misery as if it were your own, because it *is* your own— is somehow enervating, and makes one whole, or larger, or better. And that's when I knew I was headed back to the drawing board.

My time there yielded the following revelation: NOUXtrition can only work as an indefinite regimen if there is, as Loam said, "something to look forward to." So here we go: I propose biweekly Feast Days for each NOUXtrition consumer. Twice a month, they will all be summoned to a central checkpoint for pickup, after which they will be corralled, via a fleet of shuttles, to Cow Palace in Daly City, which I suggest because of its remoteness, size, and apparent uselessness to the majority of the city's populace. Once there, each consumer will be injected with a serum that neutralizes the SSS effect for twelve hours. Then they'll be provided with a decadent spread of bloody, gristly delights from which they can freely graze from dawn until dusk. No alcohol will be served, of course. Consumers will be quarantined until they've fully cycled through all stages of the conventional digestion process. I can assure you, *no one* will be reintroduced into general circulation until they're back to pooping balloons.

And with that, Supervisors, I'm going to wrap it up and let public comment commence, so we can get on with the vote. Standing before each of you right now, I feel confident that you'll do the right thing. Because when I look at your faces, I don't see skepticism. I don't see scorn. I see a new ray of understanding dawning, and it's one I've waited so long for, and it means more to me than any response I've ever gotten from any group of people, and keep in mind I once pitched to a V.C. in the middle of the Bay, on a yacht that was also its own tax-exempt sovereign nation, and if they rejected your pitch you'd get dumped at the Farrallon Islands and left to swim home through hordes of great whites like a fucking Alcatraz escapee. Needless to say, my pitch was *not* rejected. But this matters more. Because over the next few hours, I'm going to sit in this gallery and listen to seventy-seven members of our public, people I don't know from Adam, belly up to that podium and talk into a mic, for a period of time not to exceed two minutes, about something *I* created. Well, me and Glenn. Then I'm going to watch as you, Supervisor Ween, preside over this vote, calling out the names of your colleagues in turn, one after the other, eliciting a chorus of *Ayes*.

What will I do then? I won't cheer. I won't gloat. I won't indulge in theatrics. I won't shake anyone's hand. I won't even stick around. I'll walk to U.N. Plaza, and I'll sit down on the edge of the fountain, and men will come and ask me for money—*enough for a cup of coffee, enough for a bite to eat*—and I'll give it to them. All of them. I'll empty my pockets. Because the demise of a backward era doesn't begin here, in these halls; it begins out there, and I want to savor and own the ritual enactment of a barbaric custom before it disappears forever. I'll do it for Glenn. I'll do it for Loam. I'll do it for all of us who can't live like this anymore. I'll throw bills at anyone who asks and they'll wander off to stuff themselves as the pigeons gather at my feet and the fog unrolls, and I'll feel that cheap little do-gooding thrill for the last time. And then it'll ebb, as it always does, and surrounded by cold and dark, I'll bask in the glow of tentative absolution conferred on us all by an entire city's groaning, incremental acquiescence to progress. Because a thing in its final throes exudes a rare and ephemeral beauty, Supervisors; and we are crude creatures still, and there is no shame in wanting, just once, to feel it squirm, feel it writhe, feel it wage one last war between our weakening teeth.

Interview: Suzanne Rivecca

Loria Mendoza

Suzanne Rivecca is the winner of the 2016 Gina Berriault Award, an award given annually to pay homage to the eponymous writer and former professor at San Francisco State University. This interview was conducted by Loria Mendoza, the former Fiction Editor at Fourteen Hills *and a member of the award's search commitee.*

Loria Mendoza (LM): I'm thinking a lot about writers' landscapes lately, probably because I recently moved back to my hometown, Austin, after living in San Francisco for three years. I wonder, as someone who has inhabited multiple landscapes from Midwestern Michigan to the Bay Area's Palo Alto and San Francisco, if you have a writing landscape that resonates with you on such an emotional level that you find yourself unwittingly returning to that landscape, and how as a writer, do you continue to unearth new places, people, ambiguities, etc.?

Suzanne Rivecca (SR): As a writer, I've never really felt haunted by or compelled to represent or revisit a particular landscape in my work. I'm haunted more by emotional, internal terrain than by any physical or cultural landscape. In contrast, I think of James Joyce, who fled Dublin but spent the rest of his life writing about it in absentia, as an expatriate; or James Baldwin, who had to flee to Paris in order to start writing about New York. In order to identify, even unwittingly, with a particular landscape, you have to have been informed and shaped by it in some way; you have to be, even unbeknownst to yourself or in spite of yourself, a product of it, to have been permeated by it. I think writers like Baldwin and Joyce were indelibly shaped, as artists, by the physical and cultural trappings that surrounded them growing up: not just their respective cities but the religious milieu and racial/ethnic divisions and class stratifications and the burden of history that saturated them, day in and day out. Everything in their work, from diction to dialogue to theme, is suffused with those elements. I think part of it has to do with the fact that, at least for a period of time, they were able to engage with and participate in their environment uncritically, to feel somehow claimed by it in addition to staking their claim on it. At a young age, they both embodied roles that made them authorities and guides and ambassadors of sorts, representatives of their respective domains—Baldwin as a child preacher, Joyce as the eldest of ten kids—and this must have contributed to the powerful ambivalence they felt about their places of origin.

I definitely grew up in a setting rife with idiosyncratic regionalisms and cultural signifiers and religious trappings—a very small, very conservative, very ethnically homogeneous town on Lake Michigan—and I went to Catholic schools from kindergarten through twelfth grade. Strangely, though, I often feel like most of this was incidental backdrop. I wasn't connected to it, or swept up in it, or molded by it in a way that would foment preoccupation and seep into my unconscious enough to steer me to towards it as a recurring subject or obsession. My parents were New York State transplants to the Midwest, and so I think they felt similarly about the region, and I kind of absorbed that sense of quizzical remove. I always felt very detached from my physical and cultural surroundings, almost anthropologically so, and never considered myself part of a "community;" and I think that contributes to my sense of a kind of emotional statelessness where place is concerned. It's probably why I've moved around so much and felt sort of emotionally disavowed—not in a rejecting way, but as a sort of neutral default practice, as if it's just the natural order of things—by every place I've lived, no matter how fascinated or stimulated I've been by its history or culture or topography or customs or people. I think my identity, as a person and as a writer, was shaped by other things: things that were intangible and subterranean and felt somehow unapproachable and inaccessible. I was always much more haunted and defined by emotional dynamics—within my family, my school, my workplace—than by any particular setting or cultural framework or sense of collective history. My physical and cultural surroundings didn't present themselves as minefields I needed to decode or demystify or defuse in order to survive; the psychological nuances and underpinnings of every interaction and interpersonal negotiation, however, did. That's where all my energy went. In a way, this pattern echoes what has been repeatedly said about the characters in my book: that their intellectual development is more advanced than their emotional development. I could intellectualize every aspect of my physical and cultural environment, and thus put it to bed, pretty effortlessly; and I knew those aspects, if they troubled me, were things I could escape. I could always find another place to be, a more like-minded group to associate with, a more politically hospitable area to move to. But I couldn't intellectualize or escape relational dynamics, or satisfactorily explain to myself why certain things made me feel the way they did, why they loomed so large and felt so urgent, why I or anyone else was at their mercy. And I think most fiction writers are driven to write about the stuff they can't intellectualize or escape. It's what Robert Olen Butler calls the "compost" of the brain: you draw from it unwittingly, and it dictates where you go artistically. And I keep returning to a set of fundamental internal conflicts and interpersonal dynamics that, to me, are as real and as dense with associations and smells and textures and mores and rules as any physical place.

LM: I often hear fiction writers who draw elements of a story from their wells of personal experience say, "I can't write about this or that yet, I'm still too close to it, it's too raw, I need more time." When I read your stories, however, I feel submerged in wonderfully tonal complexities that are so freshly and precisely honest. There are so many different microclimates of feeling—from fear to grief to wishing you were someone else to falling in love—I feel like you're sparing no one, not even yourself, the writer. I guess my question is: Is this your mastery of the story form, of your emotions, or are you simply a witch? (I mean that as a compliment, of course!) As someone who has been writing stories since the age of five, how did your young heart cope with writing emotions then? How does it now? Is there anything that feels too close for you to write about?

SR: When I was five I was writing stories about ice cream and bunny rabbits, so writing was purely "fun" at that age, and just felt freewheeling and innocently exhilarating. And the older I got, the more intently focused I became on description: on pinning something down, like a lepidopterist, and describing it with as much laser-like exactitude as I could. At first, these things were exclusively physical and visual: sunsets, flowers, the texture and variegations of tone in someone's ponytail, the striations in a chunk of rock. Then they turned to facial expressions, how a tiny adjustment in the way someone held their face could indicate a radical change of mood or a particular response. Partly, I think this was an outgrowth of my own hypervigilance, which evolved into a defense mechanism and guidepost; but it wasn't just a therapeutic practice, this mania for describing. It was joyful and rewarding and immensely satisfying, and I just loved ferreting out the right words. I did it in the way some kids put together puzzles. And eventually I became fixated on trying to describe emotional states—how something felt internally, and how emotional responses manifested in the body; and I was fascinated by the fact that the only language available to describe ineffable emotional states was the language of tactile sensation: sadness feels heavy; anger feels hot and red; humiliation feels like a crumpling; etc. I remember playing with that aspect, trying to describe how something felt—for example, if a certain song made me feel euphoric and ennobled—in ways that incorporated the physical, and in ways that eschewed the physical.

Around ten or eleven, my writing started taking a turn that felt intensely charged and emotionally subversive—by which I mean that I was writing things that I wasn't supposed to be thinking, let alone committing to paper: emotional transcripts and imagined scenarios that I instinctively felt were taboo and unsayable and would deeply mortify me if anyone read them. At the time, I loved books like *Anne of Green Gables*, and I was writing stories that emulated the diction and setting of those books as well as their courtly avoidance of overt darkness. But I incorporated into these weird Victorian rip-off stories elements of the emotional conflicts I was experiencing in my real life. I didn't want to face any of those conflicts head-on, so I just sublimated them, folded them into the storyline of some ancillary character who'd attracted the

concern or curiosity of the beautiful, strong, resilient Anne-esque protagonist. The Anne-like character would have a fucked-up friend or a
recluse relative or an abused neighbor or whatever, and she'd have this
kindly-but-non-perverse curiosity about their plight; and so I got to
identify with her uncontaminated and exempt perspective, while still
delving into the particularities of these characters' dysfunction with a
kind of relentless exactitude. And I was very afraid of anyone seeing
these stories. Not because they were salacious or scandalous, but because, despite their Victorian trappings, they indicated such a concerted
and fixated investment in the pursuit of deciphering what was going
on around me and inside of me, emotionally and psychologically. That
investment felt somehow shameful, as if acknowledging the degree of
my vigilant attunement exposed how vulnerable I was to what the world
threw at me, how hopelessly I was held in its thrall. I realize now that
I was trying to create a language for certain feelings and dynamics that
felt urgently important to me yet stubbornly resistant to articulation.

It was around this time that I began to register the distinct impression, from my family and peers, that this was not a normal thing to do,
this practice of making things up, and of dissecting the ins and outs of
these invented scenarios as if their stakes were enormous, elucidating
them with such obsessive specificity and intimate detail. Having an inner life, in general, was not normal or desirable. And the act of writing,
which got its charge from an ever-present tension between the inner
life and the outer, was considered insular and fussy and antisocial and
vaguely creepy in its tinkering, blissed-out disassociation—or, alternate-
ly, its hyper-association—like a grown man who's obsessed with paint-
ing tiny collectible figurines or something. Something that meant you
invested the bulk of your energy and enthusiasm in a world other than
this one, perhaps because you weren't strong enough for this world, or
because you were insufficiently tethered to it. So as a child and teenager,
I was desperate to avoid admitting that I did this. It didn't feel safe. At
the same time, I felt that it comprised my entire identity, and I clung
tenaciously to that identity. And I knew on some level that it was connected to this world—that it was an indication not of estrangement, but
of the fact that I was much more entangled in this world than I would've
preferred to be.

So this is all to say that, if my stories convey a certain emotional urgency that feels raw or unprocessed or immediate or fraught, I think it's because I still carry that tension between wanting to tease out and illuminate the unsayable aspects of some experience, and wanting to protect myself by mythologizing that experience. It creates a kind of double consciousness in each story, an awareness of the temptation to let myself, as storyteller, off the hook coupled with the need to keep discomfiting myself by uncovering dark revelations. Most of the stories in that first book involve a protagonist perpetuating a delusion or deceiving herself in some way, and culminate in the hidden meanings of things catching up with her, despite herself. When a protagonist in one of my stories becomes undone, it's not because something happens to her; it's because she catches an unmistakable, disorienting glimmer of what it possibly meant, and the accompanying ramifications for her sense of self and a reordering of her belief system. I think this pattern, which manifests in almost every story I write, mimics the way my relationship with writing has developed ever since I was a kid.

⌒

LM: In your work, I appreciate the different perspectives of what I can't help but say in a perfumed whisper as, "female characters." I love the Catholic school girl protagonist in "Death is Not an Option" half-joking, half-confessing, that the Free Willy anthem of her senior year makes her want to go harpoon a whale, yet when she gets an "F" for moral ambiguity because she writes on a test that protesting abortions is a "violation of bodily integrity," I find myself protesting, Hey come on! She's morally ambiguous, sure, but not in the way you think. In, "None of the Above," when Alma swears never to "praise her girl students for their docility and her boy students for assertiveness," I can't help but do a little fist pump in the air. A feminist gave me your book to read, I think solely because I'm a feminist short story writer who wants to read things written by feminist short story writers. You've talked in other interviews about how you write about women, "not selfless, martyred, long-suffering Oprah's Book Club girls and women, but fierce, neurotic, single-minded, obsessive girls and women." What's at stake for the women you're writing about now? Do you feel that there is a certain expectation "out there" for your women characters? Is there any advice you can give to the rest of us trying to resist critical condensation and literary sexism?

SR: For the characters in my first book, the stakes were very internal. Primarily, they had to do with self-definition, how to own their actions instead of feeling like every decision and act of will was not, in fact, of their own autonomous volition but was a conditioned response. If I had to sum up all of those characters in one word, it wouldn't be "victims" and it wouldn't be "traumatized" or "sassy" or "prickly" or "damaged" or any of the other imbecilic and reductive descriptors that've been used to describe them. It would be "trapped." Trapped not by circumstances, but by some vicious internal pattern that felt, to them, predetermined and fated. The stories largely consisted of them trying to act out in ways that subverted that, while lacking the language to really name it.

In the past couple years, I've discovered the fiction of Edward St. Aubyn, and it caught me off guard: not because it depicts extremely traumatic events, which it does; but because he articulates, with astonishing clarity and dignity, that internal dilemma that has always obsessed me and obsessed my characters. This passage from his novel *At Last* sums it up: "The idea of a voluntary life had always struck him as extravagant. Everything was conditioned by what had gone before; even his fanatical desire for some margin of freedom was conditioned by the drastic absence of freedom in his early life. Perhaps only a kind of bastard freedom was available: in the acceptance of the inevitable unfolding of cause and effect there was at least a freedom from delusion."

These days, without having planned it that way, my protagonists tend to be male as often as female. I'm working on a collection of fiction that's shaped heavily by the decade I've spent working in homeless services in San Francisco. So my current characters are people of all ages are who experiencing homelessness, people working in human services, law enforcement and the media, people confronted in various ways with drug use and economic disaster and the shifting ethos of a rapidly changing city. What's happening in the city now—what's been happening here for the past five years, more or less—is extremely concerning to me and it preoccupies me on a daily basis, and I've seen it and experienced it at very close, behind-the-scenes range, thanks to the places where I've worked. It's not abstract for me. The huge and ever-widening gap between the very rich and the extremely poor in this city; the wave of gentrification that's been displacing the very people who have built these neighborhoods and lived in them for generations; the changing attitudes about what constitutes philanthropy and charity, largely shaped by the influence of the tech sector and the "sharing economy;" the way this town is governed and how certain people in it are rendered stateless, expendable, simply because they lack the representative power of richer constituents; the emphasis on "optics" as opposed to actual human aid: all of this gets under my skin and riles me up creatively because it's an outsized variation on all my old preoccupations. It's the old problem of being shaped by forces outside of one's control: only, this time, the definitions of identity are externally imposed and largely accepted by the populace as objective truths, not inwardly incubated and nurtured as secret, subjective credos. But the stories still revolve around the question of how people are defined. Who is awarded status as a person who matters, and the criteria for that, and the ways in which people justify that to themselves. As in my first book, this one also shares a preoccupation with how the state of victimhood is defined, and the expectations that exist for a "perfect victim." I'm still interested in subverting the definitions of victim, villain, savior, just in a way that's a little more Orwellian and encompasses a wider range of those roles' manifestations.

As far as advice regarding literary sexism, all I can recommend is that you question and probe people—whether they're workshop colleagues or professors or Amazon reviewers or whatever—when they say, "I can't connect with this story because the character is unlikable." If someone says that about a work of fiction, chances are very high it's written by a woman and that the character they're calling "unlikable" is female. When I was in workshop, I'd occasionally get comments along the lines of "I don't like how self-absorbed this character is; her narcissism ruins it for me," etc. Whereas people could write male protagonists who were rapists, homophobes, total shitheads and it would never occur to me to say "this character's propensity for rape REALLY makes it difficult for me to sympathize with him. Make him a nicer guy, so I'll be more comfortable." No, instead I was examining how plausible the protag's actions seemed in the context of his characterization; or I was assessing how well the author conjured his inner life and motivations. I'd be looking at craft, not judging the character morally.

As a representative example, when I was at Stanford there was one guy in my workshop—I'll call him Bob—who consistently wrote stories with very affable, easygoing, well-meaning male protagonists, men who were very "relatable" and decent and guy-next-door. Then one day he turned in a story in which the male narrator was a date-rapist who took advantage of young, ingenuous foreign girls. When it was time to work-shop this story, one of the other guys opened the session by saying, "It's just so refreshing that Bob *finally* wrote a real jerk!" Everyone seconded the sentiment. Why? Not because readers can relate to a rapist, but because Bob's protagonist finally had some complexity and ambiguity and sharp edges and moral quandaries to him. Finally, the story was grappling with something that had stakes, that wasn't just copping out emotionally by telling the tale of some nice, sad dude whose girlfriend dumped him. Bob's nice-guy stories were boring and self-indulgent, not because the protagonists were decent people, but because it was the same dynamic over and over again: some nice guy being done wrong, and the only lingering impression you were left with was, "Wow, why is everyone so mean to that poor guy? He just wants to live a simple life!" Whereas, the way Bob wrote this rapist, you could feel, whether you wanted to or not, the tortured, half-baked, fatalistic, yet horribly binding rationalizations the character made for his own behavior. It dis-comfited the reader and I'm sure it discomfited the writer. That's why everyone was like, "yay, Bob!" And no one was like, "Oh my God, is Bob actually a rapist?"

I've never, in my many years of workshop, heard anyone applaud a female writer as being brave or risky for writing an amoral or self-serv-ing or unlikable female protagonist. Instead, I've heard comments like "Maybe, in this story, the narrator could realize that plenty of people have it worse than her," or "This princess really needs a comeuppance;

she needs to *learn* something from this experience." These comments come from both women and men. No one ever said to Bob, nor would anyone ever say in reference to a sexually violent male protagonist, "This guy needs to read *Against Our Will*, STAT." Readers don't just expect likability from their female leads; they expect expiation for sins and self-realization. Instead of critiquing how the author has or hasn't created a fully realized, rounded, complicated person, they're making moral prescriptions. "This is what this character needs to do to be redeemed." Additionally, the female character is much more likely to be equated with her creator than the male character is with his. Bob was never suspected of being a rapist, but I've been suspected of being nuts or maladjusted or a devastated victim based on the characters I've written about.

I'll be the first to point out when a story itself feels misogynistic: that is, when it seems to endorse and propagate a worldview in which women aren't fully human, or are relegated to being mere accessories to a male character's epiphanies. But that's different from complaining about a character's moral deficiencies and trying to pass that off as a legitimate criticism. Fred Exley's alter-ego character in *A Fan's Notes* is one of the most misogynistic narrators I've ever read; and yet, the book itself isn't misogynist. You can see around the narrator. He's not framed as an inviolate hero; he's an absolute, toxic, self-loathing, tormented, self-sabotaging, brilliantly compelling mess. I hate the way the character treats women, but that doesn't stop me from relating to him, because he's a self-determined pariah, an outlier, an alienated curmudgeon with an underlying stratum of stormy, inchoate, yet unbearably lucid yearning that breaks my heart.

So when someone says, "I just can't relate to this story, because the character is unlikable," I'd recommend pressing them on that statement. Is the story bad because the character feels like a mouthpiece for the author's agenda, or because the badness of the character feels overdone and deliberately sensationalized to the point of caricature, or because every supporting character is cardboard-thin, or because there's an authorial resistance to exploring ambiguity and nuance and complexity in the character's inner life and relationships? Then, fine; that's just bad writing. But if the only rationale for hating the piece is "The character's a bitch," then that's bad, lazy reading. Encouraging people to articulate and interrogate and justify their own responses, to actually apply critical thinking to their own knee-jerk reactions, is one way of getting to the bottom of our collective resistance to certain kinds of characters.

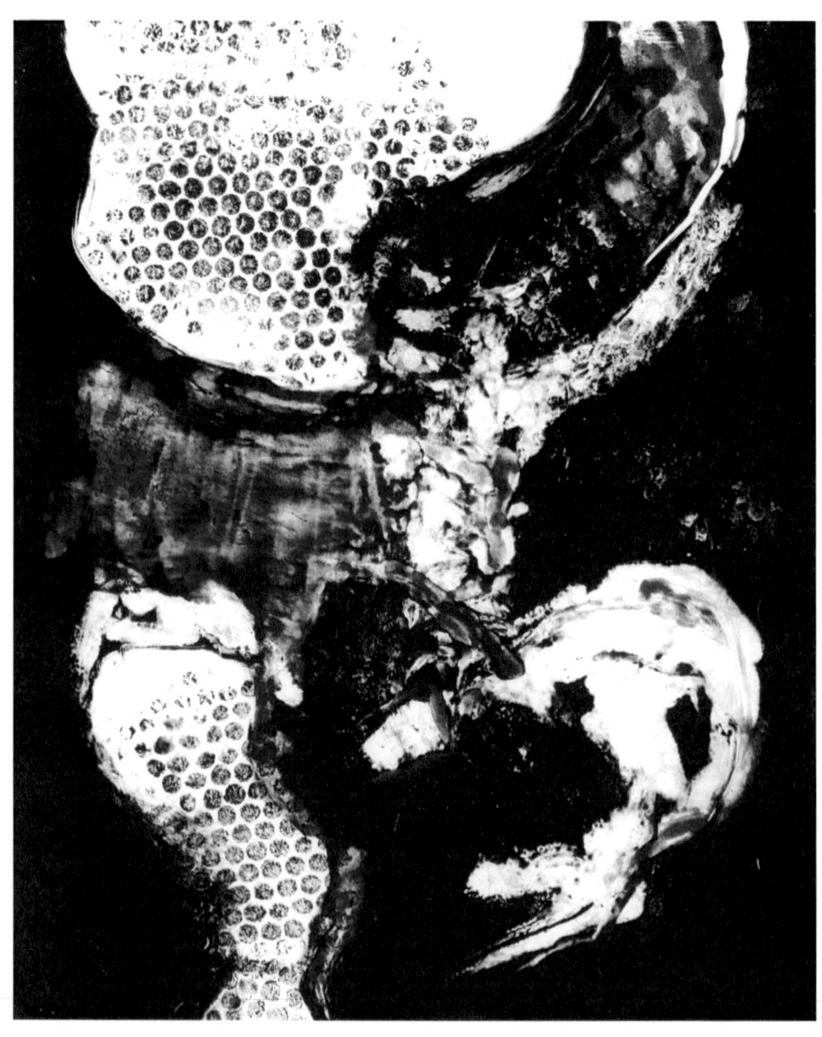

Untitled

Barry Ebner
MONOPRINT

Walls Series

Barry Ebner
MONOPRINT

I Felt the World Cracking

Megan Peak

There's a tenderness to grief
is what I keep reminding myself,
listening to sizable hail pelt the windows
of our small and cluttered apartment,
while trying to prepare my Midwestern spouse
for the routine violence of a Texan spring.
The next morning: the air like a string
of bloated pearls, the wife gone before
I rise, the bed another tomb I must pitch
myself from. My body's so incapable
today, like it was yesterday, as I drove
to grab mediocre coffee instead of making
my own. Incapable as I saw something
wrong in the road, the way it piled up
in one spot, how my throat caught
on all that yellow. The *o, o, o, o*
of my mouth. Even then I felt the world
cracking. Even then I knew—as I pulled
over and picked up their bodies, some still
flitting, yawping, some so obviously gone—
how little I could do for their cracked
beaks and flattened wings. How little
my mother could do for me as I called her
sobbing from the car and she said: *slow
down. I don't understand.* My father, too,
as I explained the lemon-yellow and silver,
the bright red secrets on each wing tip.

O, a cedar waxwing. I say it in my
head: cedar waxwing, cedar waxwing.
I want to know what about this world
is tender, but I am still in bed, now
feeling the skin on my head, picking
at it until it bleeds. The brightness
on my fingertips, the comfort in digging
away away. All I can think about
are the birds and how I should clean these
new wounds, how I must care for all
the little deaths in me.

Go to the Edge of Giving Then Break Yourself

Ösel Jessica Plante

This is the advice I get from the universe
or rather, from an astrologer who's giving
his report by a duck pond in New Zealand
talking about Mars and Jupiter, the energy
of all exotic creatures, of which the duck is not
one. Distracted, I glaze the surface of his words
like the duck nuzzling its feathers, or some algae,
or is it his partner's reflection? One duck plus
one duck equals a pastime to throw bread at, a
puzzle of innocence, reason not to say "majestic
creatures." *The new moon,* he says, *enters Sagittarius.*
My partner thinks I can never be serious, but I
want to get below, or be brought low by my
lover, to give until I'm like a holiday party after
the candles have sputtered out, after the guests
have left and the wine has set in the carpet. I'll
waddle to him on hands & knees so he can
see what he's done, plumping my feathers,
tipping over for him, pouring out until he can no
longer doubt his love. So I watch astrology
reports about how the heavens move, a science
of looking for clues. And last night he saw me
taste him in the lemon rinds I bit, taking them
off the water glass rim, *for bioflavinoids,* I said. I
need these distractions, the planets of laughter,
giving all I have to everyone I paddle past
because I can't wrap him in all this affection. I'm
trying it his way, holding back, I step by
constellations trying to make my way across his
house at night after using the bathroom, afraid to
bruise my legs on the furniture, wake him.

In the Dining Room

Lindsay Hunter

In the dining room every evening, Mr. Carter cups his hand on your ass, holds it there like his hand is the mold and your butt is the jello. And hi you this evening, he asks, his eyes twinkling but not totally meeting yours, connecting with your eyebrows instead. They don't know what they doing, he don't know what he doing, is what Tanya always says, which means Let him touch you, just get it over with, show him to his seat, get him his prune juice. Mr. Simkins can't think of the words for "iced tea." Points at a glass, says um um. When you were new you said water? Juice? Soda? We don't have soda. Coffee? Then you remembered there was also iced tea. Iced tea? And his eyes flooded with relief. One day he can't remember the word for Hello, stares at you, his lips trembling. You say Well hello there but he still looks unsure, later you hear he might have pooped his pants at the salad buffet. The sisters tell you when you're taking their order. *Genie was filling her bag,* they say. They mean the Ziplocs they bring to fill with food and take up to their rooms, where it molds and rots and stinks up the hallways, the sisters bursting into the dining room yelling *Something died, something died, I need a glass of milk!* You dated a man once who said you smelled like this place. Like mashed potatoes and floor cleaner and something else he couldn't put his finger on. Told you to shower before coming over. *Genie was filling her bag and she smelled a shit. Walter,* that's Mr. Simkins's name, *Walter was the only other person around,* the sisters say. They think they're whispering but they are talking over each other. They used to be southern belles with sweet faces and tiny wrists but now their mouths are mean, there's no other way of putting it, lips wrinkled and pale like something stretched wide for too long and wet tongues just a shade too dark. You want to say Now, Genie, ain't you the sister in diapers now? You feel protective of Mr. Simkins, this man with neatly combed hair and a delicate southern accent who has never cupped your ass or stolen from the salad buffet. Instead you say Now is that a Christian thing to discuss? Which might even be meaner to the sisters than talking about

Genie's shitpants. They look at you with the same dour faces, you've often wondered if they're triplets, and then the tiniest one says *I heard Margarita over there was a whore for the Nazis.* They mean the woman in the red lipstick and brightly colored muumuus who used to be a singer of some sort, sings to herself sometimes, the one whose dress gets caught up in her butt when she stands and does a squat-walk for a handful of steps until the dress is released. You like her, too, because of her lipstick, and because she pays no mind to the sisters, to Mr. Carter, but watches the sun set out the one picture window in the dining room, which is what you want to do most nights, too, her singing right into it and you swear when she does the sky goes pinker and pinker. We ran out of milk, you tell the sisters, and they gasp as if they've been stabbed as you walk away. You think how you lied to that man you dated, said you'd showered when you hadn't. You remember how you had to pass a drug test to work here, how you worried you wouldn't pass even though you'd never taken drugs, worried that maybe there was a part of you the test would show that you hadn't noticed before, that there'd be a phone call with bad news and a disappointed voice on the other end, and you sitting there struck dumb, not able to recall the words for Wait, hold on, you've got me all wrong.

Fuegal Requiem

M.A. Vizsolyi

whoever lived there before me painted
birds on the threshold in gold with
no eyes & i looked at those birds some
evenings & got nothing done not this

or even a phone call on his birthday
my grandfather barely intact i should
have said hello he said later just a
human measure would have stopped

the evening from going away & i
wonder where it went to at night with
nowhere to go in town just the bar
when i wasn't working but it wasn't

paradise the things closest to me moving
farther away all people go out feeling
betrayed but go nowhere they just
walk around & feel bad did it feel

bad it wasn't personal it was just the
birds were so lovely & so maddening
& the evening never made itself known
it never met me face to face

The Future of Society

Zachary Doss

Your boyfriend gives up and goes into The Business. He had been talking about it a lot lately, like one day you can't pay the power bill and your boyfriend mutters something about going into The Business, how much easier it would be if he just went into The Business. He won't leave it alone, The Business, bringing it up whenever he has an opening. "My father was in The Business," he says, "and our bills were always paid on time."

"So fine," you say, "Call your father. Go into The Business. Either do it or don't."

You expected your challenge to go unanswered but sure enough the next morning you wake up and your boyfriend is dressed like you would expect someone in The Business to dress. He looks alone and awkward in the clothes, like a little boy, and you love him through the feeling mounting in your chest that this is the beginning of some disaster, like you have already completely lost control. You do your usual morning things, brew a cup of tea, rub lotion into your hands, let the cat out. In the backyard, you chop some wood, run a mile, check on the goats. You go about your morning and you assume that your boyfriend has already gone off to work, gone off to The Business, but when you get back to the house after all that, he is still standing there, eyes vague.

"I start tomorrow," he says.

He stands in much this same fashion all through the afternoon and evening and into the night. You do the things you usually do. Before he went into The Business, your boyfriend was out of the house during the day. You don't know what he did, exactly, you assumed that maybe he did a lot of drinking and a lot of gambling to pay for the drinking, or maybe he stole cars or purses, but you've always liked terrible men and so you imagine that your boyfriend is of course up to no good, and the fantasy of him being up to no good is largely what has sustained you throughout your relationship, and with all that being said, you are unprepared for the fact that he has become furniture.

You get ready for bed. You brush and floss your teeth, and wash your hair, and file your fingernails until their edges are soft, and rub lotion into your elbows and knees, and put out fresh food and water for the cat. The whole time your boyfriend stands there, in his clothes for The Business, and you don't even know where he got those clothes, certainly not in this house, certainly not from you. In fact, you haven't paid a second of attention to The Business in your entire life, you know about it, of course, everyone knows The Business is what keeps society going, but you've never had anything to do with any of that. You are not invested in whatever it is that keeps society going, and, come to think of it, neither is your boyfriend, or at least you feel fairly certain your boyfriend is not invested in keeping society going, turning gears or the wheels of progress or sprocket factories or anything of that nature.

"Are you coming to bed?" you ask him.

"I am waiting for a call," he says. "This is how The Business works."

The call never comes, or if it does, it comes while you are asleep, and therefore you don't notice it or care very much about it. In the morning, you hear him make a cup of coffee and start the car and leave. You don't hear him shower or change his clothes or make a phone call or brush his teeth. You don't hear him let the cat out. That makes sense, as those things are your job, and so since you're awake anyway, you shower and change your clothes and make a phone call and brush your teeth and let the cat out. You feel very supportive, doing these important things so your boyfriend can focus on The Business.

You try to imagine him in The Business but your imagination can't fill in the gaps, can't quite make anything out of how little you know about The Business, and instead, you imagine him doing other things. For example, you imagine him robbing a bank, or stealing a car, or sticking a knife in another man wearing the apparel of The Business. Perhaps stealing the knifed man's watch and wallet and keys. Or, or, you imagine your boyfriend is performing some kind of espionage, that he has entered The Business in order to steal all of its secrets and sell them to the highest bidder. Or maybe he plans to release all of the secrets of The Business on a free website that everyone will access so they will know everything about The Business and the mysterious ways in which it keeps society going. You imagine that your boyfriend has gone too deeply into The Business and has trouble remembering who is friend and who is foe, and then he is discovered in his espionage by a boyishly handsome man who is also in The Business but is sympathetic to your boyfriend's intentions, whether he is working for personal financial gain or socially-responsible altruism. Your boyfriend has trouble trusting the idealistic young man from The Business, but eventually they become lovers and vow to take down The Business together.

In your fantasies, you are the person paying your boyfriend fifty million dollars for all of the secrets of The Business, or you are the open-minded tech entrepreneur who supports your boyfriend's free website of secrets. Sometimes you are the person sitting at home scrolling through the secrets of The Business on the free website your boyfriend and the open-minded tech entrepreneur built and you can feel through the layers of the fantasy that the secrets of The Business are important but fundamentally boring. You are reminded why you don't care very much what keeps society going: it isn't very sexy.

Sometimes in your fantasies, you are an ambitious young security guard who catches your boyfriend and his lover in their espionage. Sometimes you let them go, confident that The Business will no longer have any power over you after they destroy it, but in most of the fantasies, you shoot them both to death. You point your gun at them and scream that they should kiss, they should kiss each other, like they mean it, and then while they are kissing, you shoot them; you shoot them a lot, until they are very dead and also full of bullets.

Does the human body get heavier after it is shot up, you wonder? You imagine that the bullets weigh a lot.

Because you believe your boyfriend is on an important mission to bring The Business down, you begin to help him in any way that you can. When he comes home at night and stands perfectly still and doesn't move, you remove the clothes he put on for The Business and you replace them with other clothes that he can also wear to The Business. You dry clean the clothes so that your boyfriend always has something fresh to wear. You scrub him, too, just scrub him everywhere, make sure that he is clean and pink and ready for The Business. You rub lotion into his hands and elbows and knees so that his skin is soft and appropriate-looking. You give him protein shakes, for nourishment, and you find if you tilt his head just right, you can pour the protein shakes right down his throat even if he refuses to swallow. Then you discover that if you make the protein shakes coffee-flavored, he'll drink them willingly, so you do that.

Helping your boyfriend commit espionage begins to take its toll on you. Because you have dedicated so much energy to helping your boyfriend succeed in his mission, you are not doing very basic tasks around your home, like rubbing lotion into your skin or letting the cat in or checking on the goats. The cat has been loose outside for god knows how long. Maybe the cat finally got hungry enough that he ate the goats. You regret that you let something bad happen to the goats, although it seems better than something happening to the cat. Your teeth remain unbrushed and you remain unshowered while your boyfriend goes to The Business every morning and comes home every night to stand very still in a single spot in the home that you share. When he is at The Business, you become so tired that you stand very still in the exact spot where your boyfriend stands when it's his time to stand very still.

Your skin gets so dirty and dry that it turns red, and then it begins to itch and peel and you break out in strange scaly patches that cover your entire body. You look like a terrifying lizard-person and you smell horrible, although your boyfriend doesn't notice either of those things when he comes home to stand very still on the floor. Many weeks pass and you don't notice any espionage happening. You get bored standing very still in one place in your house, you are tired of feeling tired. Eventually, you stop standing very still in one place and check the Internet for secrets about The Business and find that there aren't any. Your boyfriend has not succeeded in his mission, or perhaps he is not trying, and you only imagined that part. According to the Internet, The Business is doing well, or terribly, and there are not enough people in The Business but there are too many people trying to get into The Business.

After much digging, you find a site that says the thing that really keeps society going is a secret cabal of lizard-people who only want you to believe The Business is working, but it's all a sham because what the lizard-people really prefer is control. You look in the mirror and realize you do look like a terrible lizard-person who might be part of some kind of secret cabal. There is something around the eyes and the corners of your mouth that suggests the tendency toward secrecy and even a little hint of the capacity for manipulation of world events. You have the lizard-face of a lizard-person who really likes control.

You decide to leave your home to find the other lizard-people, who will sympathize with your situation and include you in their plan to control the world. Outside, you are joined by the cat, who looks sleek and well-fed on goat, and you sentimentally declare him an honorary lizard-person. The cat joins you on your journey to find the other lizard-people, who you hope will not eat him.

When your boyfriend comes home that night to stand very still in a single spot and stare at a fixed point on the wall, you are not there to dress him and feed him and clean him, and while he doesn't seem to notice or alter his routine in any way, the next day he is a part of The Business that is functioning a little more poorly than the other parts, and every day after that, a little more poorly than before. Your house is slowly reclaimed by the landscape, your boyfriend coming home to floors covered in dirt, the power bill going unpaid. The roof disappears one day, boom, no roof, just like that. Your boyfriend stands in the sun all weekend and afterward works in The Business with leathery skin, his Business costume faded to a dusty no-color. In the room where he stands, there is now a cactus, so he stands next to the cactus. The goats come inside, track their small hoof prints through the dirt, eat bits of the cactus and hallucinate because of the cactus-juice. Your boyfriend stands next to the cactus and the hallucinating goats every night. He leaves for The Business every day. The goats see bizarre shapes and colors, the walls melting, an unfamiliar sky; they hear alien music. They stand still, all day, not moving a hoof, not even to get water, only occasionally stretching out their necks to bite off another bit of cactus. They don't move, though whether it's from fear or wonder is impossible to tell.

Contributor Biographies

Colleen Louise Barry's work has been published in *jubilat, Sixth Finch, Forklift, Ohio,* and other places. Her chapbooks are *Sunburn / Freezer Burn* (smoking glue gun) and *The Glidden Poems* (dancing girl press). She teaches at Hugo House and is founding editor of Mount Analogue. www.colleenlouisebarry.com / www.mount-analogue.com

Dani Blackman received her MFA from the University of Massachusetts, Amherst. Her short fiction also appears in *Green Mountains Review.* She was a finalist for the 2016 Reynolds Price Short Fiction Award. She lives in Seattle with her wife and son and teaches English at North Seattle College.

Kayleb Rae Candrilli is author of *What Runs Over,* winner of the 2016 Pamet River Prize and forthcoming with YesYes Books. They also serve as the non-fiction editor of the *Black Warrior Review* and are published or forthcoming in *Rattle, Puerto del Sol, Booth, RHINO, Muzzle, The New Orleans Review,* and others.

Melissa Carter is a conceptual photographer and painter whose work explores gender and socioeconomic disparities. In 2016, the Rhizome Foundation presented her exhibit Body America at the University of Kentucky. She has been published in *North of Center, Subbacultcha! Belgium,* and was a resident artist of Holler Poets Series. She lives and works in San Francisco.

MRB Chelko is the author of several chapbooks including *Songs & Yes* (sunnyoutside, 2015) and *Manhattations* (Poetry Society of America, 2014). Chelko's recent publications include *Black Warrior Review, Cincinnati Review, Crazyhorse, Gulf Coast, Slice,* and *Poetry International.* She lives in New York City.

Stephanie Dickinson's work appears in *Mudfish, Weber, Fjords, Cherry Tree, Water-Stone Review, Gargoyle,* among others. Her novel *Half Girl* and novella *Lust Series* are published by Spuyten Duyvil, as is *Love Highway*, based on the 2006 Jennifer Moore murder. *The Emily Fables* has recently been released by ELJ Publications.

Zachary Doss is a fiction editor for *Banango Street* and a volunteer screener for *Ploughshares*. His work has appeared in, or is forthcoming from, *Sonora Review*, *Passages North*, *Fairy Tale Review*, *DIAGRAM*, *Caketrain*, *Paper Darts*, and others. His short story "Bespoke" was the winner of Puerto del Sol's 2016 Contest in Fiction. Zachary received his MFA from the University of Alabama and currently lives in Houston, Texas, where he works in musical theater.

Barry Ebner is an artist primarily working in the techniques of intaglio and monotype. He is fascinated by marks and gesture, accident and chance. He received his MFA with an emphasis in printmaking from the California College of the Arts. He has occupied space in the Bay Area since 1999.

Laura Cesarco Eglin was born in Montevideo, Uruguay in 1976. She is the author of three collections of poetry, *Llamar al agua por su nombre*, *Sastrería*, and *Los brazos del saguaro*. Cesarco Eglin holds a BA and an MA in English from The Hebrew University of Jerusalem, and an MFA in Bilingual Creative Writing from the University of Texas at El Paso.

Emily Kendal Frey is the author of *The Grief Performance* and *Sorrow Arrow*. She is currently studying counseling psychology.

Kimberly Grey is the author of *The Opposite of Light*, winner of the 2015 Lexi Rudnitsky First Book Prize and published by Persea Books. Her work has appeared in *A Public Space*, *Boston Review*, *Kenyon Review*, and other journals. She was a recent Wallace Stegner Fellow in Poetry and lecturer at Stanford University.

Stephen Haynie's work has appeared in *The Kenyon Review Online*, *cream city review,* and *Gargoyle*. He lives in Columbia, Missouri with his wife and three children.

Lindsay Hunter is the author of the novel *Ugly Girls* and the story collections *Don't Kiss Me* and *Daddy's*. Her next novel, *Eat Only When You're Hungry*, will be released in August of 2017. She lives in Chicago with her husband, sons, and dogs.

Ashley Johnson is a photographer, mixed media artist, writer, and creative entrepreneur living in Winston-Salem, North Carolina. Johnson began exploring fine art photography with her first portrait series *Woven* in the spring of 2016 where she created custom masks weaving and dying florals to document her conscious transition from commercial photography into more introspective and self-exploratory portrait projects.

Catherine Jagoe is a writer and translator specializing in Spanish and Catalan. Her translations include the Amnesty International award-winning Argentine novel *My Name is Light* by Elsa Osorio and *That Bringas Woman* by the nineteenth-century Spanish novelist Benito Pérez Galdós.

Nicole Jost is a playwright and educator. Her work has been seen at Gadfly Theatre Productions, ReproRights! Theater, PlayGround, Rorschach Theatre, The Kennedy Center's Page-to-Stage Festival, and the Capital Fringe Festival. In 2015, she received the James Milton Highsmith Playwriting Award for *The Terror Fantastic*. Nicole is pursuing her MFA in Playwriting at SFSU.

Raeleen Kao is a drawer, printmaker, and amateur competitive eater aka glutton residing in Chicago with a Charles Brand etching press, a red tabby, and forty plants. Her prints and drawings have been exhibited in museums and galleries across the country. Her work has been represented at SELECT Fair New York, the Editions and Artist Books Fair in New York, the Cleveland Fine Print Fair, the LA Art Show, and Aqua Art Miami forthcoming November 2016.

Jesse Lee Kercheval is the author of fourteen books of poetry, fiction, and memoir including the poetry collections *Cinema Muto* and *Dog Angel*. Her translations include *Invisible Bridge/El puente invisible: Selected Poems of Circe Maia*. She is also the editor of *América invertida: An Anthology of Emerging Uruguayan Poets*.

Glenn Kinen was raised in Miami in a Cuban-Argentine family, attended Harvard College, and lives in Connecticut. He has been published in *Washington Square* and *No Tokens*.

Tyler Kline is the author of the chapbook *As Men Do Around Knives* (ELJ Publications, 2016) and the current poet laureate of Bucks County, Pennsylvania. He works on a vegetable farm and teaches middle school English. His recent work has appeared or is forthcoming in *the minnesota review*, *Passages North*, *Parcel*, and elsewhere. Find him online at tylerklinepoetry.com.

Krystal Languell was born in South Bend, Indiana. She is the author of the books *Call the Catastrophists* (BlazeVox, 2011) and *Gray Market* (1913 Press, 2016), as well as chapbooks and other publications. Development Director for Belladonna* Collaborative and publisher of the feminist poetry journal *Bone Bouquet*, she works as a freelance bookkeeper for small presses and an Adjunct Associate Professor in the Department of Humanities & Media Studies at Pratt Institute. Her poetry has won a 2013-2014 Poetry Project Emerge-Surface-Be fellowship and a 2014-2015 Lower Manhattan Cultural Council workspace residency. New work is forthcoming in *American Poetry Review*, *Boston Review*, *Bayou Magazine*, and elsewhere.

Alyssa Lempesis is an Oakland-based artist whose work examines uncanny ecologies, both real and imagined, and the bodies that inhabit these worlds. Lempesis received an MFA from University of California at Davis (2014) and a BA from University of California at Berkeley (2012).

Mia Ayumi Malhotra is a Kundiman and VONA/Voices Fellow, and her poems have appeared in *Greensboro Review*, *Mid-American Review*, *Drunken Boat*, *Best New Poets*, and elsewhere. She is a founding editor of *Lantern Review* and can be found online at miamalhotra.com.

Michael Mungiello is from New Jersey. His work has been published in *Eclectica*, *TXTOBJX*, *Cheap Pop*, and elsewhere.

Kristian O'Hare's plays have been produced or staged in Detroit, San Francisco, Chicago, New York City, Boston, and Los Angeles. *The New York Times* called his play *Like Poetry* "a highly promising production... beautifully structured, with an impressive blend of poignancy and humor." As a poet, his work has been published in *The Cobalt Review* and selected as a finalist in 2016's Tennessee Williams Writing Festival.

Megan Peak holds an MFA from The Ohio State University. Her work has been published or is forthcoming in *Blackbird*, *Cimarron Review*, *Indiana Review*, *Linebreak*, *Ninth Letter*, *North American Review*, *Pleiades*, *Ploughshares*, and *Verse Daily*. You can find her at www.meganpeak.com.

Kevin A. Phan is a snow plow operator who lives in Colorado. His favorite item in the kitchen is the garlic press. When reading Berryman, as you can imagine, he is equal parts giggles and tears.

Ösel Jessica Plante's poetry and flash fiction has appeared or is forthcoming in the *Best Small Fictions 2016 anthology*, *Crab Orchard Review*, *the minnesota review*, *Mid-American Review*, *Mississippi Review*, *New Ohio Review*, *Rattle*, *Salamander*, *SmokeLong Quarterly*, *Zone 3*, and others. She is pursuing a PhD in Poetry at Florida State University.

Suzanne Rivecca is the author of the story collection *Death is Not an Option*, which won the Rome Prize from the American Academy of Arts and Letters. She is the recipient of writing fellowships from Stanford University, the Radcliffe Institute for Advanced Study, and the National Endowment for the Arts. Her short stories have won two Pushcart Prizes and have appeared in *American Short Fiction*, *Granta*, *New England Review*, *Fence*, and *Best American Short Stories*. She worked in the homeless-services sector of San Francisco for many years.

Anna Rotty lives in San Francisco. She received a BFA, with a focus in photography, from the University of Massachusetts Amherst in 2011. Anna explores the tension between resistance and acceptance of change. Much of her work has a dreamlike quality, referencing memories and abstracting the familiar.

Michael Trocchia is the author of *Unfounded*, a collection of verse, and *The Fatherlands*, a chapbook of prose. His work features in journals such as *Baltimore Review*, *Colorado Review*, *Tarpaulin Sky*, and *The Worcester Review*. He teaches philosophy at James Madison University and works in the university's library.

John Sibley Williams is the author of nine poetry collections, most recently *Disinheritance* and *Controlled Hallucinations*. Winner of the Philip Booth Award, American Literary Review Poetry Contest, Confrontation Poetry Prize, Vallum Award for Poetry, and others, John currently serves as editor of *The Inflectionist Review*. He lives in Portland, Oregon.

Northern California artist **Bryan Valenzuela** lives and works in Sacramento. For over a decade he's been aiming to perfect a unique drawing technique involving the atomization of the figure by carving out shape and light with handwritten text. Though virtually unnoticeable from afar, once the viewer steps closer to each work they are engulfed in a barrage of words intermingled with other mixed media elements such as needle and thread, acrylic paint, and collage. Recent winner of both the Leff-Davis Fund for Visual Artists and a Best in Show prize at the 2015 California State Fair Fine Art Exhibition, Valenzuela was chosen by the City of Sacramento to create a large scale public art piece for the new Golden 1 Center in downtown Sacramento that was completed in October of 2016. When not working in the studio, he's composing and recording music, performing and touring with the band Exquisite Corps.

M. A. Vizsolyi is the author of *The Lamp with Wings: love sonnets* (HarperPerennial), winner of the National Poetry Series, selected by Ilya Kaminsky. He is also the author of the chapbooks *Notes on Melancholia* (Monk Books) and *The Case of Jane: a verse play* (500places press). He is part of the faculty of the BFA in Creative Writing Program at Goddard College and faculty advisor for the college's national literary journal, *DUENDE*.

Twitter:
@BerkeleyFiction

Tumblr:
BerkeleyFictionReview

berkeley fiction review
www.berkeleyfictionreview.com

MIDWESTERN
GOTHIC
A LITERARY JOURNAL

FICTION AND POETRY BY
FRANK BILL | BONNIE JO CAMPBELL | ROXANE GAY
AMOREK HUEY | LINDSAY HUNTER | JEFF VANDE ZANDE
AND MANY MORE

DISCOVER A REGION WITH A VOICE ALL ITS OWN
MIDWESTGOTHIC.COM

IR

INDIANA REVIEW

Fiction
Poetry
Nonfiction
Artwork

SINCE 1976

indianareview.org
inreview@indiana.edu